BIRDS

A GUIDE TO THE MOST FAMILIAR AMERICAN BIRDS

by

HERBERT S. ZIM, Ph.D.

and

IRA N. GABRIELSON, LL.D., D.Sc.

President, Wildlife Management Institute
Former Director, U. S. Fish and Wildlife Service

ILLUSTRATED BY JAMES GORDON IRVING

A GOLDEN NATURE GUIDE

GOLDEN PRESS • NEW YORK

FOREWORD

This book pictures in full color 129 of the most familiar American birds. Using these birds as keys, the text describes additional related and similar species, helping the reader to identify more than 250 birds in all.

The selection of the most common birds of America and the assembling of concise information about them were achieved through long, detailed study of voluminous data on our bird life. This might have been an impossible task were it not for the wholehearted cooperation and assistance of ornithologists and other naturalists. John Aldrich, C. A. Cottam, Allen Duvall, D. F. Hoffmeister, A. C. Martin, Ernst Mayr, A. L. Nelson, A. Sprunt IV, R. E. Stewart, H. L. Webster, and Alex Wetmore gave helpful comments and suggestions. Special thanks are due to Chandler S. Robbins of the Patuxent Research Refuge, who compiled the basic data for the range maps, checked migration dates, tabular data, and other factual information, and who rechecked these data for the current revision. James Gordon Irving has contributed his knowledge of birds as well as his unusual artistic talent.

In the present revision, 10 additional pages of information have been added, plus a listing of scientific names. We hope readers will find this fuller and more attractive volume more useful.

H.S.Z.
I.N.G.

Library of Congress Catalog Card No. 61-8323

HOW TO USE THIS BOOK

This is a field book made to fit your pocket when you go looking for birds. Check each range map (example below) to see if the bird occurs in your region. Concentrate on these birds. Generally, areas where birds live in summer are shown in red on the maps; winter areas are in blue. Purple shows areas where the bird is a permanent resident.

Migrating birds pass over parts of the white areas in spring and fall. Check their "time table" as given on pp. 132-153, where you will also find information on nests, eggs, and food. Mark each bird you are likely to see, and when you have seen it, record the date and place. Thumb through this book and become familiar with the birds. Then, when you see them, you'll recognize some at first sight. Also make use of the information on pp. 154-155 concerning books, museums, and places to see birds.

The more you look at this book, the more facts you'll find. The color plates show spring plumage of male birds, and sometimes females and young. The text emphasizes field markings, size, important facts, related birds which are similar in appearance, and differences between males and females. The birds have been selected so that knowing one bird will help you to know others like it.

The birds illustrated are among the most common and the ones you have the best chance of seeing. No rare birds or birds of limited range are included. In almost every part of this country you can see many of the birds pictured and described in this book—plus other common local birds you will soon learn to know.

SEEING BIRDS

You have been seeing birds as far back as you can remember and you will continue seeing them wherever you may be. It's a real pleasure to see them. You can see more birds and more kinds of birds by learning how to look. This book will help you. It is not written for the expert, but for people who want to see birds just for the joy of it.

Begin by giving your attention to the birds in your own vicinity. These are the birds to learn first. Don't try to memorize the details of size, shape, or color of head, wing, or tail. Learn to know the whole bird as one total picture, since one glance at a moving bird may be all you'll get. When you can recognize a flicker or an oven-bird, then concentrate on the markings that make it stand out: color, habits, the way it moves, its special kind of flight and—most important—its song and calls. Each of these will help you to know the bird you see.

You will find more people interested in birds than you might imagine. Sometimes they're organized in clubs. Some just get together and go looking for birds. They will be at camps, at the seashore, and in most out-of-door places. They will share whatever they know with you. If you are beginning, remember that everyone was once a beginner. If you want to identify birds, ask questions and then ask more. Before you know it, people will be coming to you with their questions.

Practice is essential. Go looking for birds as often as you can. As to time of day, early mornings are best. By the time the sun is well up, bird activity slows down and does not resume till late afternoon. Marsh birds are most active near dawn or in the evening, but ducks, waterfowl, and hawks may be seen all day. Make bird watching a week-end habit the year round. Try getting out early on spring mornings when the birds are migrating north. Follow and observe them as they nest in the summer. Watch them as they form flocks and start south in the fall. You learn something from every bird you see.

EQUIPMENT The only essential equipment for seeing birds is a pair of eyes. Good ears are a help, too. But there are ways of increasing your enjoyment, none of which involves much expense. This book is one, for a guide book is important. As you acquire experience, you will want more advanced books (see page 154). Your own records, if kept systematically, are an important part of your equipment. A pocket notebook to record detailed information is worth carrying. Old clothing, waterproof shoes, and a bottle of mosquito repellent are part of an experienced bird watcher's equipment.

Field glasses or binoculars are the most important and most expensive item of equipment. There's no denying their value in bringing tree-top birds down to you. Like a good camera, a good pair of glasses is a precision tool and should be selected with care. The best glasses are made with prisms to reduce their size. The power of the glass tells how much closer it makes a bird appear. Through 3x (3-power) glasses a bird looks three times as close. Glasses of 3x to 8x are best. Remember, the higher the power, the more limited your field of vision. Glasses that admit the most light are the best. This depends on the width of the front lens (usually measured in millimeters). A 6 x 30 lens admits more light than a 6 x 24. The large 7 x 50 glasses are excellent for birds. Glasses that adjust by a single center focusing screw are most convenient. Don't be in a hurry to buy glasses. Ask other bird watchers first; learn something of costs, for a good pair of glasses is a lifetime investment.

WHERE TO LOOK   Birds are everywhere, but to see the most birds try looking in the best places: in moist woodlands or perhaps at the edge of a wooded swamp. Young scrubby woods are likely to have more birds than mature forests. Wood margins are generally good, especially during migration. But no single place is best. Salt-water marshes and shores will yield birds that one will never find in pine woods. Other species prefer open fields, or western deserts. A wooded park in the midst of a city is one of the very best places to look for birds during migrations. If you explore your own region, you will discover certain spots are favored—perhaps a small glen with a brook, a wooded point on a lake, a marsh, or cottonwoods along a river. On page 155 is a list of some famous places to see birds. Make local inquiries. See also the books and museums listed on page 154.

HOW TO LOOK   Dashing through the woods will get you nothing but shortness of breath. Experienced watchers will often sit quietly in a likely spot and let the birds come to them. Keen-eyed birds are easily frightened by movement. Don't make yourself conspicuous against the open sky. Move slowly; and the less time spent on the move, the better. Try to cover several distinct areas, if possible—a woodland, marsh, field, river bank, shore, or whatever your locality affords. Eventually you will work out a route which will give you the greatest returns in birds seen for the time spent. Experience in your own region will be your best help. Make bird watching a year-round activity, for each season has its own special surprises and delights to offer the careful observer.

WHY LOOK? When a person is really interested, there's nothing like the thrill of seeing a beautiful bird, identifying a species you have never seen before, and watching your records grow. All of our extensive knowledge about birds has come from bird watching. We have learned something of the importance of birds in the world of wild life and know how they help control the many insects that plague us. Your own garden may not be much better off, but—by and large—birds help hold insects in check. We have discovered that a single kind of bird is neither "good" nor "bad," but that all birds from hawks to hummingbirds have their important natural place. Some birds do occasional damage; some birds are occasionally a direct help to man; but these are both exceptions and are not typical of the total picture of bird life.

From watching birds we discover more about their food and habits and so are able to do more to protect those that need help in order to survive. Perhaps you may be able to help in establishing a local bird "refuge"—an area where passing birds can rest and feed and where resident birds can nest. Once you have made a start in seeing birds, you may want to do more than just look. The section on Amateur Activities (page 16) suggests some things for you to do.

PARTS OF A BIRD

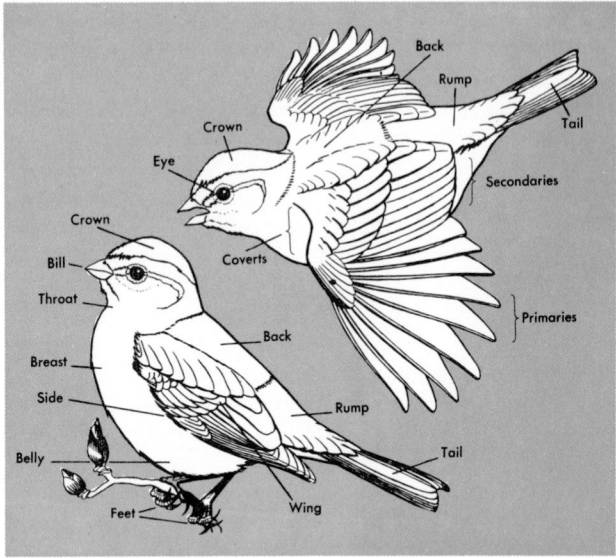

Names are tools. Bird experts have dozens of scientific names for the various parts of birds. Using these scientifically defined terms, they can describe a bird with great accuracy. The beginner does not have the experience to use these terms even if he knew them. So only a minimum of technical terms is used in this book. When you see a bird you cannot identify and want help from some expert, try to observe the bird so well that you can describe its size, habits, and the color and form of the parts illustrated above. Put your information down on paper (don't trust your memory). By keeping these few parts in mind you will systematize your observations and secure the details needed to get your bird identified.

BIRD CLASSIFICATION

Birds are grouped into orders, families, and genera according to similarities of bills, feet, and wing forms. If you know these groups, the relationship and classification of birds will be clearer. Classification also refers to body parts not important in field identification but essential in scientific study. Here are a simplified list of the main bird groups in this book and a family tree which shows their relationships. On pages 156-157 are listed the scientific names of all of the birds illustrated. These names and the common names used are based on those adopted by the A.O.U. (American Ornithologists Union) Checklist Committee.

LOONS: Large swimming and diving birds; tails short; legs set far back. Four toes: 3 front ones fully webbed. Bill sharply pointed, higher than wide. **page 21**

GREBES: Smaller swimmers and divers. Tail lacking; legs far back. Four toes with thin skin flaps (lobes) and with flattened nails. Bill slender, pointed; higher than wide. **page 22**

HERONS and BITTERNS: Long-legged wading birds. In flight, feet extend beyond tail but neck is pulled in. Bill straight and sharp; skin between eye and bill bare. Four toes, scarcely webbed or not webbed at all. Middle toenail has comb-like margin. **pages 23-26**

DUCKS, GEESE, and SWANS: Swimming birds with distinct tails. Legs centered. Birds walk well compared to grebes and loons. Four toes: front 3 webbed. Bill broad and flat, often with "teeth" along edge. Upper bill ending in short, flat hook or "nail." **pages 27-33**

CRANES, RAILS, and COOTS: Marsh birds flying with neck extended and feet dangling (rails); wings rounded. Four toes, unwebbed (except for coot, which has lobes). Middle toenail without comb-like margin (see Herons). Patch between eye and bill is feathered. **page 34**

PLOVERS, SANDPIPERS, and SNIPES: Long-legged shore birds, mostly small. Bill usually conical, long and soft; nostrils opening through slits in bill. Generally 4 toes: hind toe raised and short. Sanderlings and most plovers have only 3 toes. **pages 35-39**

GULLS and TERNS: Mostly light-colored marine birds. Wings long, narrow and pointed. Bill hooked (gulls) or pointed (terns) with nostrils opening into slits that go through bill. Four toes: hind toe small and not webbed. **pages 40-41**

HAWKS, EAGLES, and VULTURES: Large birds. Bill strongly hooked; feet powerful, claws long and curved. Vultures differ in having a bare head with nostrils connected by hole through bill. **pages 42-47**

GROUSE, QUAIL, and TURKEY: Land birds which scratch for food. Bills short and stout. Feet heavy, strong; hind toe short and raised. Wings short and rounded, with stiff feathers. **pages 48-50**

PIGEONS and DOVES: Small-headed birds with slender bills, grooved at base; and with nostrils opening through a bare fleshy area at base of bill. Legs short. Four toes: all on same level. Hind toe as long as shortest front one. **pages 51-52**

OWLS: Bills strongly hooked. A swelling at its base is concealed by feathers. Toes with large curved claws; entire leg feathered. Eyes large and immovable in puffy, feathered "face." **pages 53-55**

CUCKOOS: Long, slim birds with slightly curved bill. Tail long, feathers not stiff or pointed; central tail feathers longest. Four toes: 2 in front; 2 behind. **page 56**

SWIFTS: Small swallowlike birds; bill small with no bristles at base. Mouth wide. Wings slender and very long, reaching beyond tail; tail with 10 feathers. **page 57**

NIGHTHAWKS: Birds with large heads, small bills and wide mouths. Bill usually with bristles at base. Feet small; middle toe long with comb-like claw. Feathers soft, dull-colored. **page 59**

HUMMINGBIRDS: Tiny birds with bill slender and needle-like—longer than head. Feet small, weak. Feathers on back usually shiny green. **page 60**

KINGFISHERS: Head large and crested. Bill long, strong, pointed. Feet small and weak. Four toes: 2 of the 3 forward toes joined for half their length. **page 61**

WOODPECKERS: Climbing birds. Bill strong, pointed, with bristles at nostril. Tail feathers stiff and pointed. Four toes: 2 in front, 2 in back; or (rarely) 3: 2 in front and 1 in back. **pages 62-65**

PERCHING BIRDS: The largest bird group. Land birds, mostly small, with 4 toes—all on the same level, never webbed. Hind toe as long as middle front toe—an adaptation for perching. Tail with 12 feathers. **pages 66-127**

FAMILY TREE OF BIRDS

Birds developed from reptile ancestors millions of years ago, as internal structures and scaly legs still show. Most of the 20,000 or more bird species have become so specialized that group relationships are hard to trace.

Hawks and Eagles

Plovers and Sandpipers

Coots and Rails

Gulls and Terns

Woodpecker

Pigeons

Vultures

Herons

Quails and Kin

Archaeornis, a bird of 150 million years ago

Water-fowl

Grebes

Loons

Tanagers

Wood Warblers

New-World Finches

Old-World Finches

Waxwings

Larks

Crows and Jays

Titmice

Nuthatches

Vireos

Shrikes

Blackbirds

Flycatchers

PERCHING BIRDS

Swallows

Wrens

Kinglets

Weaver Finches

Kingfishers

Hummingbirds

Creepers

Mockingbirds

Starlings

Thrushes

Swifts

Goatsuckers

Cuckoos

Owls

Birds are classified into 27 orders. In North America 20 orders occur. These are divided into about 75 families, which encompass about 1,500 species. One can find and identify 100 or so species almost anywhere. Several states record over 400 species; California, over 500.

Tern   Loon   Heron   Kingfisher

ADAPTATIONS OF BIRDS

ADAPTATION

Birds show unusual adaptations to their way of life. The most important and obvious is a covering of feathers. These have developed from the scaly covering of reptiles. Each feather has rows of branched barbs which hook together. On the long flight feathers, the barbs mesh tightly to form a firm structure. Contour feathers and an undercoat of finer down cover the bird's body. Form and structure of feathers vary with different birds.

Internal adaptations of birds include air sacs and light, hollow bones; a very rapid heart; temperature several degrees higher than ours, and other structures favoring a very active existence. The animal food of birds includes insects, worms, mollusks, fish, and small mammals. Plant foods include seeds, buds, leaves, and fruits. Bills are an obvious adaptation related to diet. Above are four birds, each from a different family, with similar bills adapted for eating fish. This parallel development of parts is well known.

Robin— perching

Ptarmigan —feathered

Pheasant —walking

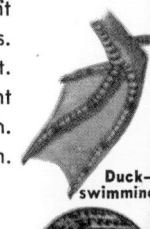

Duck— swimming

Primary Flight Feather

Barbs and barbules enlarged

vane   shaft   quill

Shrike Cardinal Wood Thrush Crossbill Yellowthroat

OF FEET

Owl—grasping

odpecker—climbing

Yellowlegs—wading

Coot—swimming

Above is a series of five birds all belonging to the same order. Each species has developed a very different type of bill suited for eating different foods. These are divergent developments from a common family ancestor. This type of development is also common.

Other adaptations are shown in the legs and feet of birds. The five-toed pattern common in most backboned land animals has been lost. The bird's three or four toes have been modified for climbing, scratching, grasping and tearing, and swimming. Long toes distribute the weight of birds that walk on mud and sand. Extra feathering protects the feet of ptarmigans and arctic owls. The long legs of waders, the webbed feet of swimmers, and other adaptations indicate specialized uses of various kinds.

Most interesting of all adaptations are those of behavior. Many species have developed distinct patterns of living. Careful observations will disclose the "personalities" of different birds and their social adaptations.

Body feather with aftershaft

Body feather

Down feather

Lewis' Woodpecker
at feeding station

AMATEUR ACTIVITIES

Everyone starts watching birds with the same ideas in mind: to learn their names, to identify as many as possible, and to see what kind of "records" his watching will yield. Some people are content doing these things and never venture beyond this stage. Others find many more ways to broaden their knowledge. Time, place, and experience will determine how far you want to go. Here are some suggestions:

Downy Woodpeckers
like suet

Bluebirds
enjoy
seed-cakes

ATTRACTING BIRDS BY FEEDING

Birds were here long before people fed them—and they will continue to feed and care for themselves. But if severe storms completely cut off the food supply of winter birds, large-scale cooperative efforts are sometimes essential to save them. It's another story if you want to attract birds to a particular place during winter—as your own yard or window. Then feeding will help. Feeding means more than scattering scraps of bread around. Find out the best way to build feeding stations. Set them near shrubbery to give birds shelter. Place lumps of suet in wire containers for creepers, chickadees, nuthatches, and woodpeckers. Small grain (sunflower seeds, hemp, millet, and canary seed) will attract seed eaters. At a window station you can watch birds feed.

ATTRACTING BIRDS BY WATERING

Birds need drinking and bathing water just as much as they need food. A watering place will attract more birds during warm months when wild food is available. Birds like moving, shallow water. A trickle of water running into a one-inch pan with gravel on the bottom is excellent. Nothing elaborate is needed. An old bucket with a drip hole hung over an old baking pan will do as well as any elaborate cement pool.

Drip-bucket provides water

ATTRACTING BIRDS WITH COVER AND SHELTER

Birds need cover for protection against wind, cold, and enemies. The best kind of cover for birds is shrubs and vines that provide food as well as a place to hide. Plants that look attractive to us are not necessarily attractive to birds. Native plants that retain their fruit in winter are best. Nesting boxes are seldom satisfactory unless they are built with a specific bird in mind. A box for a wren must be very different from one for a flicker. Get complete instructions and follow them.

Open nest-house

Wren house

Wood Duck house

Build a box that can be easily cleaned and used year after year. Don't place boxes too close; three or four nesting boxes to an acre are usually enough. Most birds set up their own "territory" and will keep other birds out.

CREATING A LOCAL REFUGE   A group of people may find a way to create a local bird refuge to help birds care for themselves. Most communities have swamp or waste-land which can easily be developed into a bird refuge. Parks, golf courses, and cemeteries have been successful. Ample water supply is needed. Small dams across a brook will create shallow ponds that attract many birds. Swamp plants and grasses should be encouraged as seed pro-ducers. Evergreens may be planted for shelter.

BIRD PHOTOGRAPHY   Hunting with a gun is giving way to hunting with a camera. Only a few species of game birds may be shot, but you may photograph any bird. Bird photography offers thrills and hard work. Don't be-gin until you really understand photography. A flash bulb is usually necessary even in daylight, because many birds prefer deep woodland shade. A fast lens is essential, too. Bird photography calls for patience, skill, and real effort, but one fine shot makes it all worth while.

Steller's Jay (13 in.), only blue crested jay of the western conifer belt

Banding a
Yellow-breasted Chat

BIRD BANDING A bird watcher soon learns the usefulness of the thin aluminum bands put around birds' legs to help in scientific field studies. From the 7 million birds banded we have learned much about migrations, flyways, life spans, movements of young, population changes, and annual returns to a place.

Cooperation of thousands of amateurs has made scientific study of birds possible. If you find a banded sick or dead bird, except a pigeon, look for a serial number, like "24-24401" or "509-30091," and for an address that may read, "F. & W. Serv. Wash. D.C." Write the number on a postcard, stating when, where, how, and by whom the bird was found. Send the card to the Bird-Banding Office, Patuxent Research Refuge, Laurel, Maryland. In reply, you will receive the history of the bird. Information you gave will help complete one more record.

Permits to band birds are issued to qualified persons by the U.S. Fish and Wildlife Service. An applicant must be at least 18 years old, and three experts must vouch for his ability to identify birds. He must be willing to accept the responsibilities that go with scientific work. The official aluminum bands and record forms are supplied free.

Color bands

Official bird bands

BIRD COUNTS AND CENSUSES As soon as you can recognize the common birds, you will begin to keep lists of species you see. This is the beginning of what may become an important hobby. As you get to know birds better, your lists will include estimates of the number of birds seen as well as the kinds of birds. The next step is to concentrate on a specific area and do a complete census. The resulting figures may give an idea of the density of the bird population there. Many bird clubs make such a count on Christmas day, and this gives a spot check on the winter bird population all over the country. Counts made during the breeding season help determine the number of adult birds per acre. This varies from 2 to 20 birds with type of land and the locality. Carefully made counts, especially those repeated year after year on one tract of land, are of real scientific value. Special counts made during migrations, counts of bird colonies or bird roosts, help us understand more about certain unusual species.

LIFE HISTORIES So much is still unknown about the way birds live that any careful observer can gather new information of scientific value. The ability to make immediate detailed records of what you see is essential, and you must continue watching and recording till the story is complete. We have so much more to learn about songs, flight patterns, courtship, nesting, feeding habits, care and training of young, behavior of males and females, etc., that there is work for all bird watchers who care to join in. During a summer vacation a well-prepared amateur can add definitely to our knowledge of some bird by observing even a few nesting pairs and recording complete data about them. Preparations for this work should include reading some of the excellent life histories of birds that have already been written.

COMMON LOON

LOONS Spot loons by their large size, long body, short neck, pointed bill, and loud, yodel-like call. Loons are expert divers, but kick along the water before taking off in flight. In winter Common Loon is gray above and white beneath. Red-throated Loon (25 in.) is a smaller species with reddish throat. Arctic Loon (24 in.) is similar to the Red-throated, but with a black throat in summer.—*Length: 28-36 in. Female similar to male.*

Common

PIED-BILLED GREBE   Grebes are expert divers and swimmers. Smaller than most ducks, they float lower in the water. The Pied-billed Grebe is darker in winter, when throat markings are lacking. It has a more rounded bill than other grebes. The Horned Grebe is the same size; head black with chestnut "ear patches." Red-necked Grebe (19 in.) is grayer, with white cheeks and a pointed, yellowish bill.—*Length: 12-15 in. Female similar to male.*

GREAT BLUE HERON, our largest common wader, flies with a slow, regular wing beat. It nests usually in colonies, but often it nests alone. Its call is a low-pitched croak. Distinct from other herons, because of its size. Common Egret (38 in.), almost as large and all white, has yellow bill and black legs and feet. Snowy Egret, definitely smaller (24 in.), is similar, with black bill and legs, yellow feet.—*Length: 42-50 in. Female and young similar to male.*

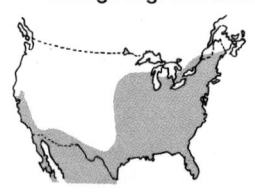

GREEN HERON This widespread heron usually lives and nests alone. A dark bird, scarcely larger than a crow, it has a typical heron flight, with slow, strong wing strokes. The Green Heron may be confused with the American Bittern or the Night Heron at a distance, but its yellow-orange legs are distinctive. It raises its crest when alarmed. Adult Little Blue Heron (25 in.) is more slender, and dark all over; young are white with dull wing tips, yellow-green legs and feet; may be confused with the Egrets.—*Length: 15-22 in. Female and young similar to male.*

BLACK-CROWNED NIGHT HERON An old tree crowned with these roosting herons is a memorable sight. These colonial birds feed their young night and day. Only La. heron is also completely white below and dark above. Young are spotted and may be confused with Bitterns. The low-pitched, hoarse "quock" is often heard at night. Yellow-crowned Night Heron, a more southern species, is similar, with black head, white crown, and short white stripe on cheek. — *Length: 22-28 in. Female similar to male.*

AMERICAN BITTERN   This bird rarely ventures outside marshes. It does not perch in the open like other herons. It hides among reeds and cattails and "freezes" when in danger. In flight, its black wing tips distinguish it from young Night Herons. The Bittern's "pumping" song is unique. The Least Bittern, much smaller (12 in.), has a dark back, buff on the wings and below; more often heard than seen; call soft like the Cuckoo's.—*Length: 23-24 in. Female and young similar to male.*

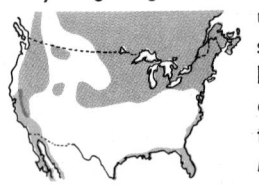

CANADA GOOSE, a very well-known and very widely distributed waterfowl, is recognized by its size, long black neck, and white cheeks. Geese swim with their necks straight up and fly, in striking V-formation, with necks outstretched. They feed in ponds but also graze on grass and sprouting grain. Several sub-species differ in size and range from the smallest subspecies (24 in.) to the large, common Canada Goose.— *Length: 35-40 in. Female similar but smaller than male.*

MALLARD This large, common marshland duck has a blue wing patch margined by two white bars. These marks identify it in any plumage. The green head and white neck ring are good field marks of the male. Mallards take off in a vertical leap and fly fast. They feed,

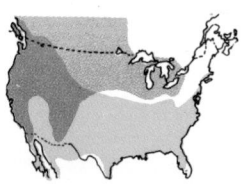 like all surface ducks, by tipping in shallow water. Mallards have been domesticated and have crossed with other ducks. — *Length: 19¼-28 in. Female smaller than male, mottled brown and buff.*

BLACK DUCK This common eastern duck resembles the female Mallard, but is darker and also has white wing linings. Males have bright-red legs and yellowish bills. Black Ducks, like Mallards, prefer fresh or brackish water. The Mottled Duck (20 in.) is very much like the Black, but is restricted to Florida and Gulf Coast. The Gadwall (20 in.) differs from the Black Duck in its smaller size, white belly, and small, rectangular white patch on black edge of the wing.— *Length: 22-26 in. Female smaller but similar to male.*

WOOD DUCK The male lacks brilliant colors during the summer, when it resembles the duller female, although its bill is always brighter. Recognize it in flight by its short neck, white trailing edge to wing, and bill held at a distinct downward angle. Wood Ducks fly low, dodging around trees, where they roost. Distinguished from American Widgeon (20 in.) in flight by lack of large, white patch on forward edge of wings. —Length: 17-20 in. Female smaller than male, duller, with white eye ring.

PINTAIL Spot the Pintail by its long, pointed tail, slender neck, and in flight by the white stripe on trailing edge of its wing. Probably our most common duck, it almost leaps into the air when taking off. It is a surface feeder, preferring fresh water with Mallards and Black Ducks. It rarely dives. The female lacks the long pointed tail. It is similar to the female Mallard and Black Duck, but without the blue patch on wing.— *Length: 26-30 in. Female smaller; lacks solid brown head.*

CANVASBACK This duck swims low in water and dives rapidly. A long bill and low, sloping forehead are distinguishing marks. In flight, note its large size, white body, and the wings far back on the body. Flight often in long V-formations. The Redhead (20 in.) is similar at a distance, but is a smaller bird and has a darker back and an abrupt forehead.—*Length: 20-24 in. Female with olive head and neck.*

MERGANSERS are loonlike birds with narrow, cylindrical "toothed" bills. They fly low, prefer open water; dive when frightened. In flight, note the white on wings. The Common Merganser (above) is conspicuously white with a small crest. The Red-breasted Merganser (22 in.), rufous breast and larger crest, prefers salt water. The smaller Hooded Merganser (18 in.) has a fan-shaped white crest.—*Length: 21-27 in. Female smaller, gray with reddish head and feet, sharply defined white throat.*

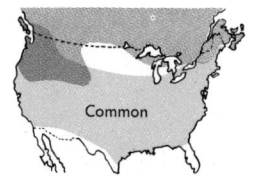

Common

AMERICAN COOT lives in marshes and along rivers. Coots are the only ducklike birds with a chalky white bill. Coots are close relatives of the gallinules, which are slightly smaller in size. Both swim with a pumping motion of the neck. The Coot's white bill contrasts with the Common Gallinule's red one. Coots dive rapidly but, when frightened, skit over the water with feet and wings.—*Length: 13-16 in. Female very similar to male.*

KILLDEER, a large plover, is marked by a double breast band and (in flight) by its orange-brown rump and tail. It frequents open meadows and plowed fields, where its loud "killdeer" call often resounds. The Killdeer bobs its head as it walks. The young leave the nest almost as soon as hatched. The Semipalmated Plover (7 in.) is similar in color to the Killdeer, but with only one breast band. It prefers mudflats and beaches.— *Length: 9-11 in. Female nearly identical with male.*

COMMON SNIPE This shy bird of meadows and open fresh-water swamps rises high in the spring air and circles with an unforgettable "drumming" sound; otherwise it keeps well concealed. Field marks are pointed wings, very long bill, rather short legs, and zigzag flight. The plump American Woodcock of woodlands and dry fields, a close relative, has rounded wings and a richer brown color. The Dowitcher (11 in.), of mudflats and beaches, has white rump and in spring is reddish beneath.—*Length: 10¼-11¾ in. Female similar to male, larger.*

GREATER YELLOWLEGS This gray-and-white sandpiper is one of the largest and most conspicuous of our shore birds. In flight, note its size, the white rump and tail. Its black, slightly upturned bill and long, bright yellow legs are the best field marks. Prefers marshes and mud banks to open beaches. The Lesser Yellowlegs (10 in.) is very similar, with a shorter bill. Willets (16 in.) are larger birds, with dark legs and conspicuous black-and-white wing markings in flight.— *Length: 13-15 in. Female larger, but similar to male.*

SPOTTED SANDPIPER   The Spotted Sandpiper is the only one with a strongly spotted breast—but the spots are present in the breeding plumage only. In many inland localities it is the most common shore bird, and the only breeding sandpiper. It typically teeters up and down

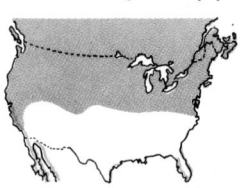

as it walks. The Solitary Sandpiper (8 in.) is similar, but with a white eye ring and white on sides of tail. Both these sandpipers have dark legs.— *Length: 7½-9 in. .Female practically identical with male.*

LEAST SANDPIPER Best known and smallest of the small sandpipers, this is a bird of mudflats and salt marshes. Note its small size, light brown back, greenish legs, and slender, straight bill. The Semipalmated Sandpiper (6 in.), found with the Least, has a grayer back, stouter bill, and black legs. The Western Sandpiper (6½ in.) has a longer, heavier bill. The White-rumped Sandpiper (7½ in.) is larger, with a distinct white rump.—*Length: 5-6½ in. Female very similar to male.*

HERRING GULL, most common of the gulls, is abundant along the Atlantic Coast and parts of the interior. It is a great scavenger. Immature birds are dull gray-brown, becoming lighter with maturity. Adults have gray wings and back, black wing tips, and flesh-colored legs. The Ring-billed Gull, similar but smaller (19 in.), has dull yellow legs and a black ring on its bill. Laughing Gull (17 in.) in the East and Franklin's Gull in West have black head and darker back. California Gull resembles Ring-billed Gull.— *Length: 22½-26 in.*

California   Herring

COMMON TERN   Terns are smaller than gulls, more graceful, with forked tails and slender wings. They plummet headlong into the sea after fish. Common Tern is distinguished by its colorful bill, dusky wing tips, and deeply forked white tail. Arctic Tern (15 in.) is slightly grayer, with redder bill and shorter legs. Forster's Tern—lighter bill and wing tips, grayer tail—and Roseate Tern (both 15 in.)—slender black bill, tail more deeply forked—resemble Common Tern.—*Length: 13-16 in. Female similar to male; young with darker bills.*

COOPER'S HAWK is typically a bird of the woods, rarely soaring in the open. Its short, rounded wings and long, rounded tail make it easy to identify in flight and also allow it to maneuver in thick brush. The Sharp-shinned Hawk is similar, but smaller (12 in.), with a square-tipped tail and lighter crown. Goshawk, larger than Cooper's (23 in.), has light gray breast, dark gray back, and white line over eye.— *Length: 14-18 in. Female larger; young with streaked breast.*

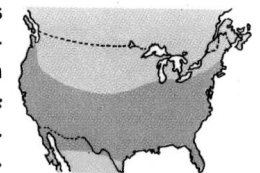

RED-TAILED HAWK The Red-tail is a large, soaring hawk. Its wings are broad and its tail, fan-shaped and chestnut-red above, is not always visible. This hawk is light underneath with dark streaks across the belly. Red-shouldered Hawk is similar with a distinctly banded tail. Other soaring hawks include the small Broad-winged Hawk (16 in.) of the East with its prominently barred tail; and Swainson's Hawk (21 in.) of the West with its broad, dark breast band.—*Length: 19-22 in. Female larger, but similar. Young with dark, faintly barred tail.*

TURKEY and BLACK VULTURES, valuable scavengers, are protected in some states. They soar in wide circles. Turkey Vultures hold their long wings slightly above the horizontal line. The naked red head completes identification of adult Turkey Vultures. The smaller Black Vulture is a more southern species with round, white patches on

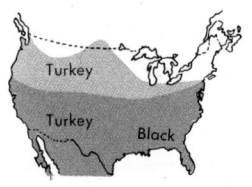

the underside of its wing tips. It has a dark head (as do the young Turkey Vultures) and a very short, square tail.—*Length: Turkey—26-32 in. Black—24-27 in. Female same as male in both species.*

SPARROW HAWK This is the smallest U.S. falcon—a hawk with long, pointed wings. Note the rich reddish-brown on its back, tail, and crown. The female's tail has narrow black bars. The Pigeon Hawk, slightly larger (12½ in.), lacks the reddish patches and has heavy black bars on the tail. The Peregrine Falcon, a less common but wide-ranging species (17 in.), has black mustache marks, a long thin tail, and pointed wings. Peregrine Falcons are trained for hunting birds and rabbits.—*Length: 8¾-10¾ in. Female slightly larger.*

BALD EAGLE Eagles are large, long-winged hawks. They soar with their wings horizontal (vultures, with their wings slightly raised). The white head and tail mark the adult Bald Eagle. Younger birds are dark-brown all over. Eagles are frequently found near water, as fish is their favorite food. The Golden Eagle (30-43 in.) of the West is dark, except for the white base of its tail and white near the wing tips.—*Length: 30-34 in. Female larger, otherwise similar.*

OSPREY The Osprey or Fish Hawk resembles the Eagle, but is distinctly smaller and slimmer with much white beneath. No other large hawk has as much white below. It flies with a decided backward bend at the "elbow" of the wing. The huge nest of the Osprey is similar to the Bald Eagle's. A group of nests is a sight to remember. The birds wheel and soar over the sea, plunging feet foremost after fish.—*Length: 21-24½ in. Female and young similar to male.*

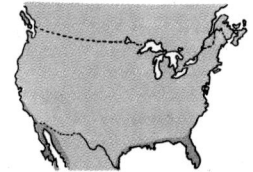

RING-NECKED PHEASANT This unmistakable Asiatic bird was successfully introduced in the West and is now found over much of the United States. It is a favorite game bird of farmlands, where it feeds on waste grain, occasionally causing local crop damage. The handsome male is unrivaled in its splendid coloring. The female is smaller, dull brown, with a shorter but also pointed tail, which distinguishes it from Ruffed Grouse and Prairie Chickens.—*Length: 33-36 in. Female smaller, duller brown and white.*

RUFFED GROUSE This is an attractive, chickenlike bird of the deep woods. It suddenly springs into the air with a whirring beat of wings. The drumming of the male is part of the spring courtship. The fan-shaped tail with its broad, dark terminal band is the best field mark. The Prairie Chicken (18 in.) of the midwest is somewhat similar but with a dark, rounded tail; it prefers open country. Several other grouse are found in the West and North.—*Length: 15½-19 in. Female smaller, duller.*

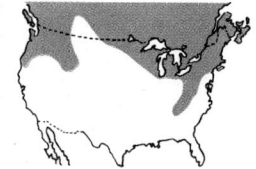

BOBWHITE Everyone knows the Bobwhite's call, but these small quail are hard to see in dead grass and weeds. Their size, ruddy color, and stubby appearance make Bobwhites easy to identify. Hunters prize them as game. Western quail (Calif., Scaled, Gambel's, Mountain, and Harlequin) are about the same size as the Bobwhite, but differ in appearance. All these western quail have some kind of plume on their heads.—*Length: 9½-10¾ in. Female larger than male; duller coloring.*

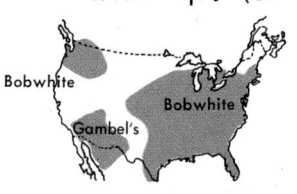

PIGEON Pigeons, variable in color, are descendants of the wild Rock Dove of Europe. Though handsome birds, their nesting habits make them undesirable in cities. The common pigeon has a broad, fanlike tail. The large western Band-tailed Pigeon (15½ in.) has yellow legs and a light band on top of the tail. The White-crowned Pigeon of Florida is a dark pigeon with a whitish crown. The tiny Ground Dove (6¾ in.) of the extreme South has a short black tail and rufous flight feathers.—*Length: 11-13 in. Sexes similar.*

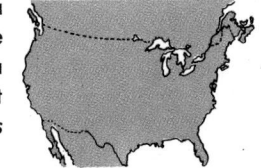

MOURNING DOVE Slimmer than the pigeon and with a long, pointed tail, the Mourning Dove nests in every state. It is named from its melancholy call: "Coo-ah, coo, coo, coo." The white tail border is conspicuous in flight. The White-winged Dove (12 in.) of the West is somewhat similar in appearance, but has a large white wing stripe.

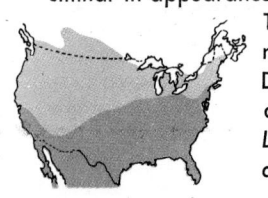

The southwestern Inca Dove (8 in.) resembles a miniature Mourning Dove. Doves are seed and fruit eaters and are prized as game birds. — *Length: 11-13 in. Female duller, with a shorter tail.*

SCREECH OWL The only small owl with eartufts, this owl is found in two color phases: a gray and a reddish brown. Like most owls, this is a bird of the night, when its descending wailing call is heard. The real "Screech Owl" is a European bird. Keen eyesight and noiseless flight enable our Screech Owl to prey on field rodents. The Burrowing Owl (9 in.) of the prairies and the Saw-whet Owl (8 in.) of the Northeast and the Northwest lack the distinct eartufts of the Screech Owl.—*Length: 8-10 in. Adults and young similar.*

BARN OWL   The long-legged Barn Owl is unique. Its white, heart-shaped face and dark eyes are unmistakable. No other owl has this facial pattern. In flight the light buff plumage is conspicuous. Color varies from bird to bird, some being quite dark. The Barn Owl, which nests in barns, belfries, and hollow trees, is important in controlling rodents injurious to orchard and garden crops. It has no close relatives but has a world-wide range.—*Length: 15-21 in. Adults and young similar.*

GREAT HORNED OWL, aggressive and powerful, resembles an overgrown gray Screech Owl. Its call is a deep, penetrating hoot, repeated five to seven times. In flight it looks like a large-headed neckless hawk. The smaller Long-eared Owl (15 in.) has similar eartufts. The eastern Barred Owl (20 in.) and the western Spotted Owl (19 in.) have dark eyes and lack eartufts. The Barred Owl gives eight hoots; the Spotted, three or four.—*Length: 18-25 in. Female much larger.*

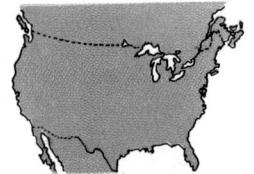

YELLOW-BILLED CUCKOO This slim, brown-and-white cuckoo is dovelike in appearance. It rarely lays eggs in the nests of other birds like the European cuckoo. Cuckoos are among the few birds that eat hairy caterpillars. The Yellow-billed Cuckoo has a yellowish under-bill, chestnut-

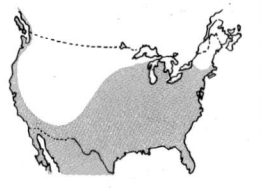

brown on wings, and conspicuous white tail spots. The Black-billed Cuckoo, similar in size, lacks the yellow bill and chestnut wings; its tail spots are indistinct.—*Length: 11-12½ in. Adults and young similar.*

CHIMNEY SWIFT   These birds are almost always in the air, flying with a batlike flight. Their short, spiny tails prop them against the inside walls of chimneys when resting. Distinctive, streamlined birds, swifts usually fly in groups and migrate in large flocks. There are three western swifts: Vaux's Swift (4½ in.) similar to the Chimney; Black (7¼ in.) and White-throated (7 in.) Swifts— both larger and each colored as its name implies.—*Length: 4¾-5½ in. Adults and young similar.*

WHIP-POOR-WILL When resting on dead leaves the Whip-poor-will is almost invisible—more often heard than seen. It flies little except when feeding. A rounded tail (white-tipped in the male) and absence of white in the wing are features that distinguish it fairly clearly from the Nighthawk. Chuck-will's-widow (12½ in.), of the South, is larger, with buff on the throat and under the tail. Poor-will, a western species, is smaller. (7½ in.) and grayer.— *Length: 9-10¼ in. Female smaller.*

COMMON NIGHTHAWK, a close relative of the Whip-poor-will, is darker and has a longer, slightly forked tail. In the air, note its distinguishing white wing spot. Nighthawks are constantly in the air, flying in a zig-zag path, circling, diving, and banking as they feed on flying insects. The Lesser Nighthawk (8½ in.) of the Southwest is very similar, with white band nearer tip of wing. It is a low-flying bird.—*Length: 8¼- 10 in. Female smaller, lighter, and without white band on tail.*

60

RUBY-THROATED HUMMINGBIRD These eastern hummingbirds are gems of beauty and marvels in flight. They hover motionless, can fly backward, and may be attracted to brightly-colored tubes of sugar water hung in gardens. Western hummingbirds include the very similar Broad-tailed (4½ in). of the Rockies; Anna's (4 in.), crown and throat of metallic red; the Black-chinned (3¾ in.), black chin and purple throat band; and the brown-backed Rufous Hummingbird (3½ in.).—*Length: 3-3¾ in. Female and young white-throated.*

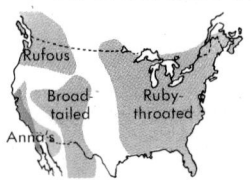

BELTED KINGFISHER Where there are fish there are Kingfishers, beating the air in irregular flight, diving into water with a splash and emerging with fish in their beaks. Note the ragged crest, heavy black bill, and harsh, rattling call. The tiny Green Kingfisher (7 in.) of Southern Texas has a dark green back.— *Length: 11-14 in. Female shown here; male lacks chestnut sides and breast.*

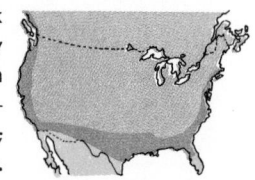

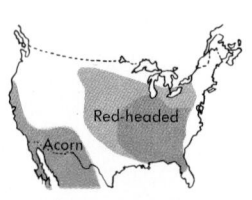

RED-HEADED WOODPECKER The only eastern woodpecker with a completely red head. The solid black back and large, white wing patches are good field marks. The Acorn Woodpecker (9½ in.) has a black back, black chin, and black breast band. The Red-bellied Woodpecker (10 in.) of the Southeast has horizontal black and white barring across the back; back of neck and entire crown are red. Woodpeckers can cling to vertical trunks, propped by stiff tail feathers.—*Length: 8½-9¾ in. Adults similar.*

YELLOW-SHAFTED FLICKER, large and brown, is identified by its bobbing flight, white rump, golden wing linings, and black breast band. Often observed on the
ground hunting ants. Like all woodpeckers it nests in a
cavity of a dead trunk or branch. The western Red-shafted
Flicker (13 in.), red under wings, has
a red mustache mark. The two flick-
ers have crossed. Hybrids may occur
in the Midwest.—*Length: 12-13 in.*
Female and young similar, but adult
female lacks black "mustache" at
base of bill.

YELLOW-BELLIED SAPSUCKER The Sapsucker feeds on the soft inner bark and sap of trees on farms and in woodlots and open woods. Sapsuckers dig row after row of small holes, sometimes girdling the tree. Note the vertical white patch on the black wing. The Pacific subspecies of the Yellow-bellied is similar, but with head and breast solid red. In the Northwest, Williamson's Sapsucker is slightly larger, mostly black, with a white rump and large white wing patch.—*Length: 7¾-8¾ in. Female smaller, lacks red on throat.*

DOWNY WOODPECKER The Downy and the Hairy Woodpecker are both common and nearly identical except for size. The Hairy is larger by some 2 in. and has a much heavier black bill. Both males have a small red head patch, lacking in the females. The vertical, white stripe down the back is a field mark worth noting for both. The Downy feeds with chickadees and nuthatches in winter, and often visits feeding stations for seeds, crumbs, and suet.—*Length: 6¼-7¼ in. Female smaller; lacks red on head. Young like adults.*

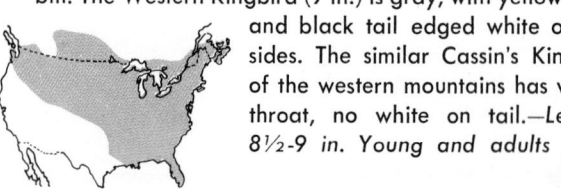

EASTERN KINGBIRD darts from its perch on a branch or fence after insects in true flycatcher fashion. The white tip of the tail marks eastern species. The Gray Kingbird (9 in.) of the Southeast lacks this, is paler, with an oversized bill. The Western Kingbird (9 in.) is gray, with yellow belly and black tail edged white on the sides. The similar Cassin's Kingbird of the western mountains has whiter throat, no white on tail.—*Length: 8½-9 in. Young and adults alike.*

GREAT CRESTED FLYCATCHER is the only large eastern flycatcher with a reddish tail. The yellow belly and wing bars should be noted as good field marks. It is an orchard and forest bird which typically uses shed snake skins in its nest. It may be confused with the Western Kingbird, except for the reddish tail. The similar Ash-throated Flycatcher (8 in.) replaces the Great Crested Flycatcher in the West.—*Length: 8-9¼ in. Young and adults similar.*

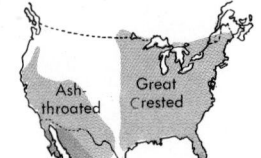

EASTERN PHOEBE If the persistent "phoebe" call doesn't identify this bird, its equally persistent tail-bobbing will. It is an inconspicuous gray flycatcher, with no good field marks. It returns to the same nesting site year after year. Say's Phoebe (7½ in.) is a western bird with rusty breast and belly. Eastern Wood Pewee (6 in.) looks like a phoebe with two distinct wing bars; it does not bob its tail.—*Length: 6¼-7¼ in. Adults similar. Young with dull wing bars.*

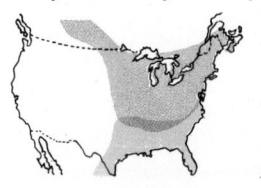

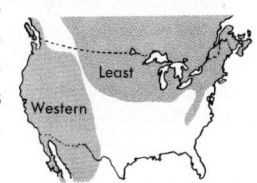

LEAST FLYCATCHER is the smallest eastern U.S. flycatcher. Note the two whitish wing bars and the eye ring. It is hard to tell this flycatcher from others in the East— Acadian, Traill's (found in West also), and Yellow-bellied. The last has a decided yellowish tint. The Acadian is the only one of these nesting in the Southeast. In the West and equally hard to identify are Hammond's, Gray, and Western Flycatchers. Simply call all small flycatchers "Empidonax"— the group's generic name.— *Length: 5-5¾ in. Young and adults similar.*

HORNED LARK Flocks of Horned Larks feed in bare fields and along shores, walking as they feed. Note black collar, yellowish throat, black tail, and, at close range, the "horns." This and European Skylark are true larks. The Meadowlark is a Blackbird. The Water Pipit (6½ in.), unrelated to the Horned Lark, is sometimes taken for it. The

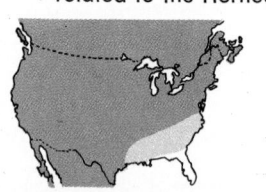

Water Pipit also walks, but with bobbing tail; head brownish, faintly streaked; outer tail feathers white.— *Length: 6¾-8 in. Female duller, young streaked.*

PURPLE MARTIN The Martins are the largest and most conspicuous of the swallows. Males have a violet head and body grading into black on wing and tail. In flight their wings are more triangular than other swallows'. Martins nest in colonies and make use of Martin houses. The Rough-winged Swallow (5½ in.), which nests singly, often in holes in gravel banks, has a plain brown back and no violet markings.—*Length: 7¼-8½ in. Female has grayish breast and white belly. Young with grayish breast.*

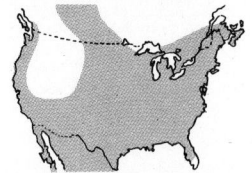

TREE SWALLOW Unbroken blue-black above and unbroken white below makes the Tree Swallow a striking bird, especially when large flocks gather to migrate in the fall. Young birds are brown-backed, but have entirely white underparts. This swallow varies its insect diet with 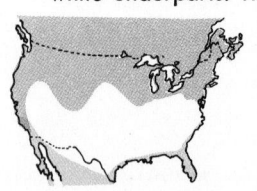 bayberries for which it has a persistent appetite. The western Violet-green Swallow (5½ in.) is similar with a white patch on each side of its rump.—*Length: 5-6¼ in. Female duller.*

BARN SWALLOW This is the one swallow with a *deeply* forked "swallow tail." Note the chestnut forehead and throat, and the buff undersides. The only other swallow with similar color is the Cliff Swallow (5½ in.), with short, squared tail, buff rump, and white forehead. The Bank Swallow (5 in.) is a brown-backed bird with a brown band across its white breast. Swallows are usually found near water.—*Length: 5¾-7¾ in. Female duller and with shorter tail.*

MAGPIES No other bird resembles the large black-and-white Magpies with their sweeping tails. There are two species—the Black-billed and the Yellow-billed—distinguished chiefly by their bills. The Yellow-billed Magpie (17 in.) lives in the valleys of central California. Magpies fly and feed in flocks. Their mixed diet includes fruits, melons, and other crop plants. They often live around ranches, and occasionally these relatives of the Crow become serious local pests.—*Length: 17½-21 in. Females similar to male.*

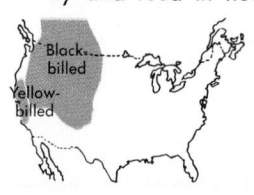

CROWS People often confuse two related birds with the all-too-familiar Common Crow. The coastal Fish Crow (17 in.) is similar except for its short nasal call: "car, car." The large Common Raven (24 in.), rare in the East, has rough throat feathers and a distinct croaking call. It soars in flight, showing clearly its wedge-shaped tail.—*Length: 17-21 in. Female somewhat smaller.*

BLUE JAY No other eastern bird is like the noisy Blue Jay, with its striking blue, black, and white color. Of the western jays, Steller's (13 in.) has a black head, throat, and breast, and long black crest. The short-tailed, crestless Piñon Jay (11 in.) is dull blue with a darker crown. The Scrub Jay (12 in.), found commonly west of the Rockies and in Florida, has a blue cap, back, wings, and tail, and a dull blue necklace across the whitish underparts.— *Length: 11-12½ in. Young similar.*

WHITE-BREASTED NUTHATCH Nuthatches creep down tree trunks head first. The White-breasted Nuthatch (white sides of head, throat, and breast) is the common eastern bird. The smaller Red-breasted Nuthatch (4½ in.) has dark line through the eye, and orange-brown underparts. The Brown-headed Nuthatch (4½ in.), of southeast pine woods, has a chocolate cap. The Pigmy Nuthatch (4½ in.) of the West has a dull gray cap, enclosing the eyes. Nuthatches often feed at feeding stations.—*Length: 5-6¼ in. Female and young duller.*

BLACK-CAPPED CHICKADEE This plump Chickadee needs no introduction. Its call is its name. The Chickadee, a constant visitor to feeding stations, often feeds upside down. The smaller (4½ in.) Carolina Chickadee—south of the Mason-Dixon Line—has four or five notes in its whistled song instead of two or three. The brown-capped Boreal Chickadee (5 in.) is a winter visitor along the Canadian border. The western Chestnut-backed Chickadee has a dull brown cap and a bright chestnut back.—*Length: 4¾-5¾ in. Female and young similar.*

TUFTED TITMOUSE There is nothing outstanding about this pert, gray woodland bird except its crest. No other small gray bird has this ornament. It's distinguished from the Chickadee by its lack of a bib and from the Nuthatch by its stubby bill and perching habit. The chestnut flanks are a confirming mark. The Plain Titmouse (5½ in.) of the West lacks this, but is otherwise similar. The western Common Bushtit (4 in.) is a nondescript gray-brown bird with a long tail, a dull brown cap, but no crest.—*Length: 5½-6½ in. Young and adults similar.*

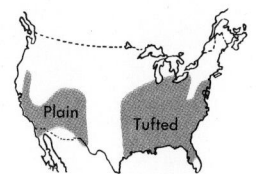

BROWN CREEPER This is the only small, brown tree-creeping bird. Its undersides are white, its tail stiff. It always works up the tree in a spiral, searching for insects and grubs, which it digs out with its curved bill. Then it flies to the base of the next tree and creeps up again. The male and the female look alike, and since their colors blend well with bark, these birds may be difficult to detect. Creepers prefer open, mature woodlands, nesting under loose bark—sometimes in old woodpecker holes. They feed in small flocks in the company of woodpeckers, chickadees, and kinglets.— *Length: 5-5¾ in. Young and adults similar.*

HOUSE WREN Wrens are small, pert, brown birds which usually carry their tails almost vertical. The House Wren is best known. It is a brownish bird which lacks distinct head markings. The Winter Wren (4 in.) has a darker belly, shorter tail, and light line over the eye. The long-tailed Bewick's Wren (5¼ in.) also has a white eye stripe, and tail with faint white border. Carolina Wren (6 in.) has a large white eye stripe and a ruddy back. Western Wrens include Cañon Wren (5½ in.) with white breast and throat and dark belly, and Rock Wren (6 in.) with faint breast streaks and white or buff-fringed tail.—*Length: 4¼-5¼ in. Young and adults similar.*

MOCKINGBIRD "Listen to the Mockingbird . . ." goes the song, and the Mockingbird is, indeed, worth hearing. Its song imitates other birds' songs, with something original added. Mockingbirds nest around homes. In the West, they are even common in the streets. They are slender, gray, and have white patches on the wings and on the tail. The Loggerhead Shrike (9 in.) is a chunkier bird with a thicker bill and a black mask across the eyes.—*Length: 9-11 in. Young and adults similar.*

CATBIRD Not quite as attractive as the Mockingbird, the Catbird sings almost as well. Its name comes from its mewing call. It prefers shrubs and vines, often near houses. Catbirds are slaty-gray, except for a black cap and a chestnut patch at the underside base of the tail. No other birds are quite like them, though some female blackbirds are grayish. Catbirds usually raise two broods a season. The male aids considerably in their care.—*Length: 8¼-9¼ in. Young and adults similar.*

BROWN THRASHER One of eight related birds, these thrashers have long tails and curved bills. They feed and nest near the ground. The handsome Brown Thrasher is a rich chestnut above and streaked with brown below. The California Thrasher (12 in.) is dark brown and unstreaked; no wing bars, Le Conte's Thrasher (11 in.) is an ashy-gray-backed desert bird with a plain, whitish breast. In the far West, the heavily streaked Sage Thrasher (8½ in.) has white tips on its outer tailfeathers.— *Length: 10¼-12 in. Female similar to male.*

ROBIN This bird's average length (10 in.) is a standard to which other birds are compared. One of the most common native birds of the East, it is the largest of the thrushes —a relationship seen in the spotted breasts of the young. Two or three broods are raised each year. Homesick colonists named the Robin after a European bird with a much redder breast. The Varied Thrush of the Pacific coast states is similar to the Robin, but has a dark breast band.—*Length: 9-10¾ in. Female similar but duller, breast paler.*

WOOD THRUSH These thrushes are typically woodland birds, recognized by their chestnut-brown backs,
redder heads, heavily spotted breasts, and clear, flute-
like song. The Hermit Thrush (7 in.) and the Veery (7 in.)
also have bright red-brown backs. The Veery has a uni-
formly colored back and only a few faint spots on its

breast. The longer-tailed Brown
Thrasher may be confused with the
Wood Thrush, but its breast is
streaked instead of spotted and its
eye is yellow.—Length: 7½-8½ in.
Young and adults similar.

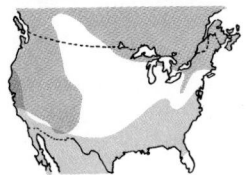

HERMIT THRUSH Famous songster, the Hermit Thrush reverses the Wood Thrush pattern. Its tail, which it slowly raises and lowers, is redder than its back. The breast is less spotted than the Wood Thrush's, but more than the Veery's. Hermit Thrush is a common and widespread bird. Other thrushes have dull, olive-brown backs. Swainson's Thrush (7 in.) has a buff eye ring and buff cheeks. The Gray-cheeked Thrush (7 in.), an eastern migrant, has gray cheek patches and no eye ring.—*Length: 6½-7½ in. Young and adults similar.*

EASTERN BLUEBIRD is an early spring migrant in the North. It is a thrush also, as the faintly spotted breast of the young testifies. Though other birds are blue, none has the chestnut brown breast of this species. The Western Bluebird has a chestnut patch on the back as well. The adult male Mountain Bluebird of the Rockies has a blue back, pale blue breast, and white belly. Bluebirds are often attracted to the correct type of nesting box.— *Length: 6¼-7¾ in. Female and young much duller.*

Western

Eastern

BLUE-GRAY GNATCATCHER With its long, white-bordered tail, the Gnatcatcher looks like a miniature Mockingbird. It is seldom seen, because of its preference for tree tops in moist woods. The blue back and white eye ring aid identification; so does the bird's habit of jerking its tail. The Black-tailed Gnatcatcher (4½ in.) is a western desert species with a black cap, less white on the tail, and a generally duller color than the Blue-gray Gnatcatcher.—*Length: 4-5 in. Female grayer, tinged with brown.*

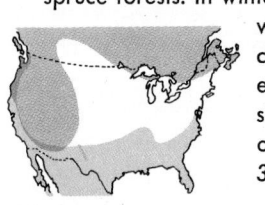

RUBY-CROWNED KINGLET This kinglet is plainer than the Golden-crowned. Its red crown is often hidden, except when the male is angry. Its large white eye ring and wing bars distinguish this kinglet when its ruby crown does not show. Both kinglets are nervous in flight and when feeding. In summer, kinglets breed in Northern spruce forests. In winter they are often found in company with Brown Creepers, nuthatches, chickadees, and Downy Woodpeckers. Kinglets are frequently seen in shrubbery about buildings, and at outdoor feeding stations.—*Length: 3¾-4¼ in. Female lacks red crown.*

GOLDEN-CROWNED KINGLET The kinglets are among our smallest birds and are doubly attractive because they are usually winter visitors. Their small, chunky bodies, stubby tails, and dull, olive-gray color are distinctive. The Golden-crowned Kinglet is the more showy of the two American species. The female has a golden crown bordered with black and white. The male has an orange stripe through the center of the golden crown. These kinglets are commonly seen feeding on the branches of firs, spruce, and other conifers.—*Length: 3-4¼ in. Female with yellow crown.*

CEDAR WAXWING These warm-brown, crested birds cannot be mistaken, especially when a flock is feeding on cherries or mulberries. Watch for the wide yellow band that tips the tail. The grayer Bohemian Waxwing (8 in.) of the Northwest has a bright cinnamon patch underneath, at the base of its tail. Bohemian Waxwings occasionally

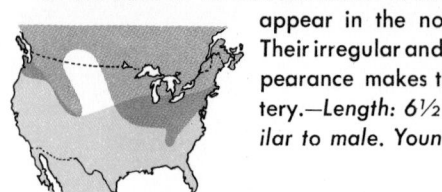 appear in the north central states. Their irregular and unpredictable appearance makes them birds of mystery.—*Length: 6½-8 in. Female similar to male. Young streaked below.*

LOGGERHEAD SHRIKE Shrikes feed on insects, rodents, and even small birds. They often hang their prey on thorns or barbed-wire fences. Resembling mockingbirds slightly, the shrikes are heavier, have a black eye mask and a hooked bill. Their peculiar bounding flight is worth noting. The Northern Shrike is a larger species (10 in.) and has a faintly barred breast; its black mask is divided by the bill, which is light on the underside. It is seen only during winter months.— *Length: 9-9½ in. Female similar to male. Young browner.*

STARLING Introduced into New York in 1890, Starlings have been spreading ever since. In some places they are a nuisance and even a pest. But Starlings are handsome birds, given to musical song and mimicry. Sunlight on their plumage makes a rainbow of colors. Note the short tail,

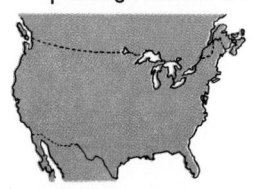

plump body, and (in spring and summer) yellow bill. Younger birds are uniform brown with dark bills, and adults (in winter) are speckled with white.—*Length: 7½-8½ in. Female similar to male.*

Yellow Warbler

WARBLERS

There are 109 species of American warblers. Fifty-six of these occur in the United States and include some of our most beautiful birds. Over twice as many warblers are found in the east as in the West. Next to the sparrows, they are the largest family of American birds and to many people the most exciting to watch. Most warblers winter in the tropics. As they migrate North, many rest and feed high in the trees and so are not easily seen, though an experienced watcher may see as many as 25 kinds of warblers on a warm May day if he searches enough. The warblers' songs may be hard for the novice to distinguish, but once known, they help considerably in finding and identifying these birds.

Warblers are small, characterized by their straight, slender bills. Their food is mainly insects, which they catch on trees or on the wing. In spring the bright colors of the males are striking. Females are usually not as brightly colored. In fall, when warblers move south, they are harder to recognize in their dull, autumn plumage. Among those likely to be seen in winter in the East, north of Florida, is the Myrtle Warbler. It winters in bayberry bushes on the coast, as far north as Massachusetts.

YELLOW WARBLER The Yellow Warbler is the only warbler that is practically all yellow and has yellow spots on the tail. Closer observation reveals the chestnut-streaked breast. The Yellow Warbler prefers shrubs or

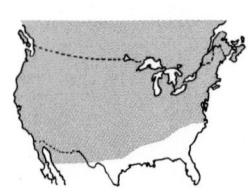

low trees and so is easily seen. The female Hooded Warbler of the southeast is similar to the Yellow, but has white tail spots.—*Length: 4¾-5¼ in. Female and young lack breast spots.*

BLACK-AND-WHITE WARBLER Only two eastern warblers are striped black and white; the common Black-and-white and the Blackpoll (5 in.), which has a solid black crown and is seen only during migration. The Black-

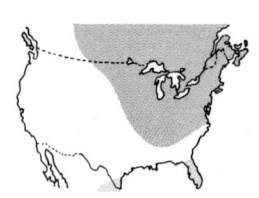

and-white Warbler stays close to tree trunks and heavy branches. The western Black-throated Gray Warbler is somewhat similar.—*Length: 5-5½ in. Female and young lack black throat.*

BLACK-THROATED BLUE WARBLER Here is a really descriptive bird name. The blue-gray back, black face and throat, and white belly clearly mark this trim warbler. No other warbler has this bold color pattern. The Black-

throated Blue is typically a bird of the open woodlands. The Black-throated Green Warbler (5 in.) of the East has a yellow-green back and golden face.—*Length: 4¾-5½ in. Female olive-brown with small white spot on wing.*

YELLOWTHROAT This is a warbler of marshes and wayside shrubbery. The black mask and yellow throat mark the male. The female has the yellow throat but no mask. Its whitish belly and absence of wing bars help

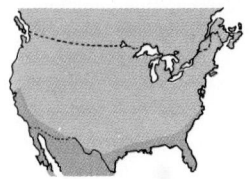

identification. The Kentucky Warbler (5½ in.) of the southeastern woodlands has a large yellow eye ring, more black on the head, underparts entirely yellow.—*Length: 4½-5¾ in. Female duller; no black mask.*

OVENBIRD Another ground-loving warbler often seen walking on the ground, its tail bobbing. The Ovenbird is somewhat like a small thrush in appearance: olive-brown above, with a striped breast. The orange crown with black

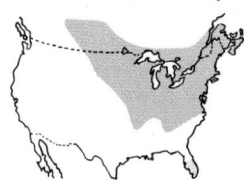

borders and a distinct eye ring make identification positive. Its often-repeated "teacher" song is as easy to learn as any.—*Length: 5½-6½ in. Female similar to male. Young lack orange crown.*

WATERTHRUSH These plump warblers stay close to the ground in swamps and along brooks. The Northern Waterthrush has a distinct yellowish cast to the heavily marked underparts, and a yellowish eye line. The more

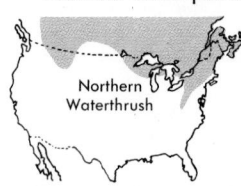

Northern Waterthrush

southern Louisiana Waterthrush is white where the Northern is yellow. It lacks the streaked throat. Both species teeter like miniature sandpipers.—*Length: 5-6¼ in. Female and young similar to male.*

MYRTLE WARBLER   The yellow rump, crown, and sides mark the Myrtle Warbler. The Myrtle migrates earlier in spring and later in the fall than any other common eastern warbler. The yellow-rumped Magnolia Warbler (5 in.) of the East has a black-streaked yellow breast, much white in tail and wings. Audubon's Warbler (5 in.) of the West is very like the Myrtle, but with a yellow instead of a white throat.—*Length: 5-6 in. Female and young browner; less yellow on crown and sides.*

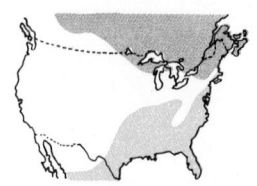

AMERICAN REDSTART   The male, black, with orange wing and tail patches, is a striking bird. The female is duller, with yellow instead of the orange and with white underparts. The pattern is unmistakable. Redstarts continually flit about, flycatcher fashion, feeding on insects.—*Length: 4½-5¾ in. Females and immature males smaller, duller, with yellow wing and tail patches.*

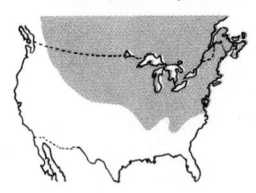

WILSON'S WARBLER (or black-capped)   A small, very active warbler, unbroken yellow below, duller above. The male has a black cap which is lacking in the female. The female is a nondescript yellow bird with no other markings. This species, which prefers moist grounds and swamps, is much commoner in the West, where it breeds in the high mountains, than in the East.—*Length: 5-5¾ in. Female lacks black cap.*

RED-EYED VIREO Vireos are a bit larger and less active than warblers. The Red-eyed has a gray crown bordered with black, a broad white line above the eye, and no wing bars. The Warbling Vireo has a paler eye line. The pale yellow eye ring and two wing bars of the White-eyed Vireo (5 in.) help to identify it. The Yellow-throated (6 in.) of the East and the blue-headed Solitary (6 in.) Vireos are like the White-eyed, but differ in their markings.—*Length: 5½-6½ in. Female identical with male; young with brown eye.*

HOUSE SPARROW This bird, misnamed English Sparrow, is not particularly a native of England and definitely is not a sparrow. It is actually a weaver finch. Imported from England in 1850, it became established, spread rapidly, and is now a serious pest. The House Sparrow may be easily confused with our native sparrows. The gray crown and black throat of the male are characteristic, as are the unstreaked crown and broad buff line over the eye of the female.— *Length: 5½-6½ in. Female duller and lacks black.*

BOBOLINK The male, entirely black below, is easy to identify. But the female and the male in winter are very sparrowlike in appearance, with buff breasts and black and buff stripes on the crown. In the South, the Bobolink, known as the Ricebird, may do serious damage to the

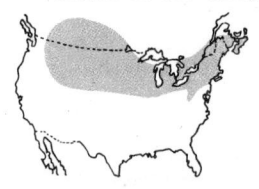

rice crop. The other grains it eats are of negligible value. The melodic song aids identification when the birds are hidden in tall marsh grasses.—*Length: 6¼-8 in. Female and male in fall are sparrow-like.*

MEADOWLARKS thrived as more land was farmed, for they are birds of meadows and grain fields. The only other large birds with white outer tail feathers are the mockingbird and shrike. Watch for the black V on the Meadowlark's yellow breast. The Western Meadowlark (9 in.) is slightly paler than the Eastern Meadowlark with more yellow on the sides of its throat. Its song is louder and more musical than the simple whistle of the eastern bird.—*Length: 9-11 in. Female smaller, darker, and duller.*

BREWER'S BLACKBIRD This is the Blackbird of western ranches and corrals. The yellowish eye of the male and the purplish tinge to its black feathers are field marks. This bird walks with its wings slightly drooping. The female is brownish gray with brown eyes. The Rusty Blackbird (9 in.), of the East, is a similar, pale-eyed bird but with a distinct rusty tinge. The female is gray and has a blue and green sheen.—*Length: 7¾-9¾ in. Female smaller, browner; dark eyes.*

REDWINGED BLACKBIRD No other bird resembles the male with its red shoulder patches with buff margins. The female, lacking this distinctive shoulder mark, is a dusky brown with a heavily streaked breast. The Tricolored Blackbird (8 in.) of the Pacific coast has even deeper red shoulders with a white margin. Both species are marsh birds, nesting in reeds and cattails. They gather in large flocks during fall, winter, and spring.—*Length: 9-10 in. Female brown; no shoulder patches.*

BALTIMORE ORIOLE The brilliant male is a showy bird. The female is a dull orange-yellow with two pale wing bars. Bullock's Oriole (8 in.) of the West is like the Baltimore but has orange on sides of head and over eye. The Orchard Oriole (6½ in.), east of the Rockies, is also similar, but with chestnut, not orange. The female Orchard Oriole resembles the female Baltimore but is greenish-yellow instead of orange-yellow.— *Length: 7-8¼ in. Female and young dull orange-yellow, with wing bars.*

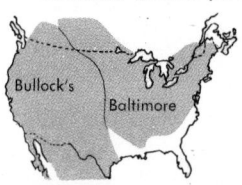

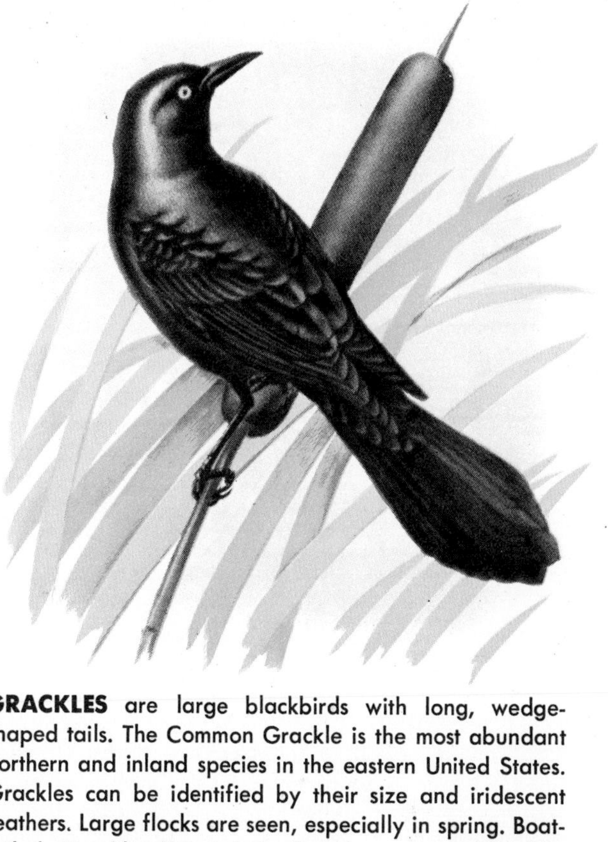

GRACKLES are large blackbirds with long, wedge-shaped tails. The Common Grackle is the most abundant northern and inland species in the eastern United States. Grackles can be identified by their size and iridescent feathers. Large flocks are seen, especially in spring. Boat-tailed Grackle (16 in.) is found along the coast from Delaware south. In Florida and south Texas it occurs inland in marshes and along rivers.—*Length: 9½-12 in. Female smaller and duller.*

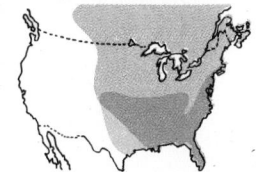

BROWN-HEADED COWBIRD has the unusual habit of laying one or more eggs in nests of other birds. The eggs hatch in ten days—sooner than those of most other birds. With this start the fast-growing Cowbirds monopolize the nest. The Cowbird is our smallest blackbird, and the only one with a brown head. The fe-

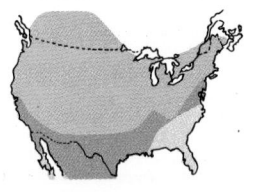

male is brownish-gray. Cowbirds walk when feeding, holding their tails higher than other blackbirds.— *Length: 7-8¼ in. Female smaller, brownish-gray all over.*

SCARLET TANAGER Identification of this unmistakable bird is obvious. The female is a dull yellow-green, smaller in size, with a heavy bill and no wing bars. The Western Tanager (6½ in.) is bright yellow with red only on the head, and black wings, back, and tail. The male Summer Tanager (7½ in.) of the southeast is entirely red; the female is orange-yellow without wing bars; the extra large yellow bill of this bird is conspicuous.—*Length: 6½-7½ in. Female smaller, dull olive and yellow.*

CARDINAL We have very few red birds—and the Cardinal is the only one with a crest. No other bird resembles it. Its heavy red bill, with black around the base, is a good field mark. The light-brown female Cardinal has the crest and red bill of the male, but very little of its color. In recent years it has gradually ranged northward. Pyrrhuloxia (8 in.) of the Southwest is gray, with red face, crest, breast, tail, and the general form of the Cardinal.—*Length: 7½-9¼ in. Female much duller. Young like females but darker.*

ROSE-BREASTED GROSBEAK The male Rose-breasted Grosbeak, nearly all black and white, flashes a deep rose patch on its breast. Like all grosbeaks, it has a heavy, conical bill. The female is a mottled yellow-brown and white, like an overgrown sparrow. The Black-headed Grosbeak (7 in.) of the West has orange-brown under-parts, and black head and back. The Evening Grosbeak (8 in.) of the North is a brilliant metallic yellow with black-and-white wings and tail. —*Length: 7-8½ in. Female mottled yellow-brown.*

114

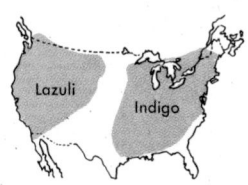

INDIGO BUNTING This is our only small bird that is entirely blue. It lives in shrubbery and cut-over woods. The southern Blue Grosbeak (7 in.) is much larger, with chestnut bars on its wings. Other buntings are splashes of brilliant color. The Lazuli Bunting (5½ in.) of the West is similar to the Indigo, but has white bars on wings and a chestnut breast. The male Painted Bunting (5 in.) of the South is a showy mixture of red, blue, and green; but the female is plain greenish above and yellowish below.—*Length: 5¼-5¾ in. Female and young uniform gray-brown.*

Lazuli

Indigo

AMERICAN GOLDFINCH The yellow body, black forehead and wings mark the American Goldfinch. In the air, the American Goldfinch is easily recognized by its roller-coaster flight and its clear song. It is a bird of fields and meadows, feeding and nesting near the ground. In the West, the Lesser Goldfinch (4 in.) is similar, with black crown, but darker (green to black) back and duller yellow on the breast. Goldfinches are close relatives of our native sparrows and, like them, are birds of open weedy fields.—*Length: 4½-6 in. Female and male in winter dull yellow-brown, with wing bars; no black on head.*

PURPLE FINCH These small, sparrow-like birds prefer pine woods and open canyons. The male is old-rose in hue; females are dull as any sparrow. Both have heavy bill, pale line over the eye, and sharp-forked tail. These finches were more common in the East before the House Sparrows drove them out. In the West, the Purple Finch and the similar Cassin's Finch (6 in.) are hard to distinguish from the House Finch or Linnet (5½ in.), but the latter is grayer-crowned and has fine, dark streaking on the sides.—*Length: 5½-6¼ in. Female of similar pattern, but entirely brown and white.*

HOUSE FINCH This bird is as common in some areas of the West as the House Sparrow is in the East. It is also a bird of farms, highways, and inhabited areas wherever water is available. The male has more brown on wings and breast than the Purple Finch. The forehead is more red than purple. The female is a nondescript, streaked bird, generally paler than the female Purple Finch. The novice should be wary of both these females—at least as far as identification is concerned.—*Length: 5½-6 in. Female smaller, paler and duller.*

RUFOUS-SIDED TOWHEE The Towhee may be identified by its "chewink" song and by its plumage. The black back and tail (white tip), white belly, and chestnut side patches are good field marks. The eyes are bright red, except in the Southeast, where they become white. A western form is very similar to the eastern species, but with white spots on the wings and back. All Towhees are ground birds, often seen scratching vigorously for insects in dead leaves.—*Length: 7½-8¾ in. Female smaller with brown instead of black.*

BROWN TOWHEE This western Towhee is as plain brown a bird as any. It has traces of reddish-brown on the throat and under the tail. The shy Abert's Towhee (8½ in.) of the desert is quite like the Brown Towhee but is more of a chestnut-brown, with a ring of black at the base of its bill. The Green-tailed Towhee (6½ in.) of western mountains is a green-backed bird with reddish crown, white throat, and gray underparts.—*Length: 8½-10 in. Female similar but duller.*

SLATE-COLORED JUNCO This even-gray bird with clear white outer tail feathers is usually seen on the ground, feeding on seeds. The female Junco is browner and more sparrowlike. There are many similar western juncos, many of which cannot be easily identified in the field. Their heads are generally darker and they usually

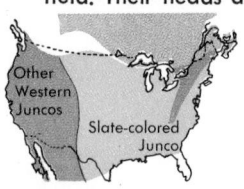

have a rusty streak on the side. The White-winged Junco (6½-7 in.) of the plains states is larger and is the only junco with two white wing bars. —*Length: 5¾-6½ in. Female smaller, browner.*

Chipping Sparrow

SPARROWS

The sparrow family also includes the finches, grosbeaks, buntings, and juncos. Altogether these make up the largest family of birds in the world and the largest family in this country, also. About 90 species have been recorded in North America. Some sparrows are very aggressive and adaptable birds. They seem to thrive in places where other birds find it hard to hold their own. The group is considered most "advanced" because sparrows are the most "successful" of the perching birds.

Sparrows are small to medium-sized, usually with stout, conical bills, well suited for crushing seeds, which are the principal item in the sparrows' diet. Seed eaters have a better chance for winter survival than insect eaters, so sparrows are common winter residents in areas where insect eaters cannot get food. Sparrows that live in the fields and near the ground are striped, brown and gray birds, easily concealed by their surroundings. They are fairly difficult for the beginner to identify. Tree-dwelling members of the family are likely to be more brightly colored. Some sparrows are good singers. The domesticated Canary (from the Canary Islands) is a member of the sparrow family.

FIELD SPARROW This is a sparrow that displays a reddish-brown crown, but to clinch its identification look for

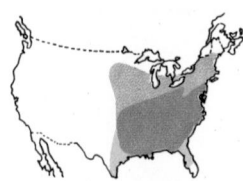

the plain breast, indistinct wing bars, and pink bill. No other small sparrow has this mark. It generally resembles the Chipping and Tree Sparrows—with which you should make comparisons. — Length: 5-6 in. Female similar to male.

TREE SPARROW The combination that identifies the Tree Sparrow includes a large black spot in the center of the grayish breast; two white wing bars; a reddish cap,

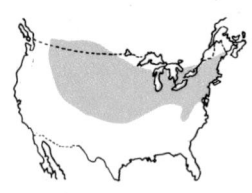

and (upon close inspection) a bill that is dark above and yellow below. Despite their name they prefer overgrown fields and roadside shrubs. Breed in the Canadian Arctic. Migrate in small flocks.—Length: 5¾-6½ in. Female and young similar.

VESPER SPARROW The white outer tail feathers are the distinguishing mark of the Vesper Sparrow. Otherwise the bird resembles the Song Sparrow. Other small birds with white outer tail feathers (pipits and juncos) are distinctly different. The Lark Sparrow (6 in.) of the West

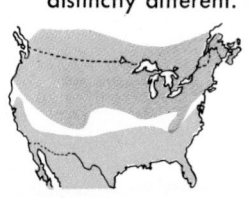

is somewhat similar, but with a white fringe around the tail, a large, bright chestnut ear patch, and a single black breast spot.—Length: 5½-6¾ in. Female and young similar.

CHIPPING SPARROW This small sparrow is equally common in the East and West. Its reddish crown, white line over the eye, black line through the eye, and black bill are good field marks. Breast not spotted or streaked. Of all the native sparrows, the Chipping is most fond

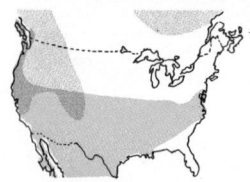

of inhabited areas, often nesting in hedges or shrubbery.—*Length: 5-5¾ in. Female similar. Young and adults have streaked crowns in fall.*

WHITE-CROWNED SPARROW Here is a sparrow worth seeing. The black-and-white erect crown can't be missed. This, the erect posture, and the gray breast with no throat markings set the White-crowned Sparrow off as a handsome bird. The related Golden-crowned Sparrow

(6½ in.) of the Pacific states is similar, but with a dull-yellow crown bordered with black.—*Length: 6½-7½ in. Female similar; young with brown head stripes.*

WHITE-THROATED SPARROW The crown of the White-Throated Sparrow is almost identical with that of the White-crowned, but you will also notice the yellow spot in front of the eye, which the White-crown lacks. Besides, as expected, the White-throat has a distinct

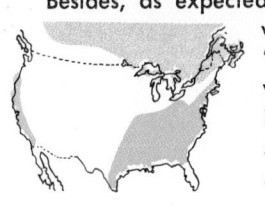

white throat patch. It is the reputed "sweet singer" of the sparrows. Its whistled "Peabody" song is a familiar one.—*Length: 6¼-7¾ in. Female similar; young with brown head stripes and less yellow.*

SONG SPARROW   A large brown center spot on an otherwise streaked breast, and a rather long, rounded tail, which it pumps up and down as it flies, are the field marks of the Song Sparrow. Its melodious, varied song, heard most frequently in early spring, is easy to recognize. Song Sparrows are birds of hedgerows, shrubbery, and

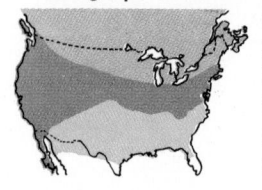

fields. Lincoln's Sparrow (5½ in.), most common in the West, is similar but with a buff breast band crossed by fine dark streaks.—*Length: 6-6¾ in. Female similar to male; young with finer spotting.*

SWAMP SPARROW   For field identification note the Swamp Sparrow's white throat, red-brown crown, plain gray breast, and rounded tail. Other sparrows with this

reddish crown are the Chipping, Field, and Tree. The Swamp Sparrow is a stocky bird without wing bars. It lives, as its name implies, in swamps and along lake margins.—*Length: 4¾-5¾ in. Female similar; young duller.*

FOX SPARROW   A large sparrow, recognized in the field by its bright red-brown tail. Its breast is heavily spotted. Though somewhat similar to the Hermit Thrush in size and markings, the Fox Sparrow has a heavier bill

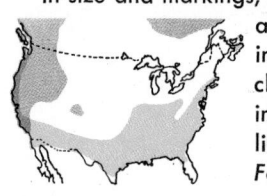

and larger, browner breast markings. It is a bird of fields and open clearings. The Fox Sparrow scratches in dry leaves with both feet at once like a Towhee.—*Length: 6¾-7½ in. Female and young similar.*

MIGRATIONS OF BIRDS

Arctic Tern (15 in.): grayish; red bill; black cap.

No one knows just why birds migrate, but many do. Heredity, instinct, secretions of glands, and responses to light may be involved. Food supply seems more important than temperature. Most shore and water birds migrate; so do many insect-eaters. Not as many seed-eaters are migrants. There are few physical differences between birds which migrate and the others. Some birds migrate by day, others by night.

Migrations north and south are best known. Some birds move only a few hundred miles from their breeding to

ATLANTIC FLYWAY

Snow Goose (36 in.), largest and most easterly of the Snow Geese. Note black wing tips.

MISSISSIPPI FLYWAY

Ring-necked Duck (18 in.) has peaked head and dull neck ring. Black above, white wing patch.

their winter range; others cover several thousand. Scarlet Tanagers travel from Peru to northern U.S. and back. Some wablers, vireos, and flycatchers travel even farther. The champion migrant is the Arctic Tern, for some of these breed in the Arctic and winter in the Antarctic, 11,000 miles away. They travel over 25,000 miles a year and cross the Atlantic in their migration.

Four North American flyways form connecting paths between northern breeding grounds and wintering areas in the southern United States, Mexico, Cuba, and South America. Their use by waterfowl is best known, though most migrating birds use them. Flyways overlap in the breeding grounds, though each tends to have its own population.

The periods of spring and fall migrations are the best

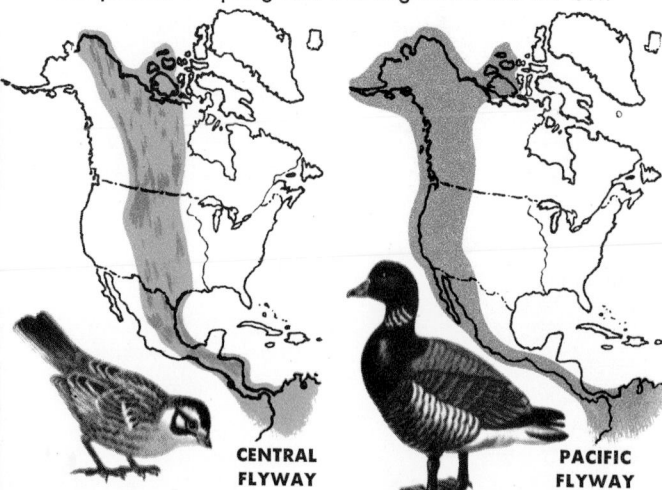

CENTRAL FLYWAY

PACIFIC FLYWAY

Smith's Longspur (6½ in.), sparrow-like, buff; white-edged tail, black-bordered cheek patch.

Black Brant (25 in.) is a small goose, dark above, with a black breast. White patch on the neck.

Varied Thrush (10 in.), Robin-like, black bar on orange breast.

Pine Grosbeak (9 in.), largest finch; white wingbars, heavy bill.

times to study birds. See pages 131-153 for more about migrating birds and when to see them.

Besides north and south migrations, vertical ones occur in high mountains. Permanent residents nest high among spruce and fir in summer, later moving down to foothills and valleys for more plentiful food. Young birds move down before cold weather. Sometimes species normally migrating farther north breed near mountain tops.

Another pattern is shown by some young eagles and herons. Soon after they can leave the nest, they start moving. By late summer or early fall many are hundreds of miles north of their breeding grounds. Toward winter they go south again.

Left: **Common Egret** (38 in.), a large heron, all white; black legs, yellow bill. Right: **Little Blue Heron** (25 in.), smaller than Great Blue (p. 23). Legs greenish. Young white; blue tint on wings.

THE BIRDS AT A GLANCE

The data on individual birds on pages 21-126 are supplemented by tables on pages 132-153. These give concisely, for each bird illustrated, a wealth of facts on migrations, eggs, nests, and feeding habits.

The information on bird migrations is given by key cities: DC—Washington, D.C.; NY—New York; B—Boston; StL—St. Louis; SF—San Francisco; P—Portland, Ore. It is usually pertinent for a radius of 100 miles. You can estimate the arrival of birds in your region from dates for the nearest key city. There is about a week's difference between DC and NY and between NY and B for most migrating birds.

Birds found in an area the year round are listed as "permanent residents." Others come north in spring, stay all summer, and depart in the fall. For these "summer residents" (SR), the table gives the average date of arrival and departure. Such birds may be seen at any time between the two dates—and sometimes a bit earlier or later. Other birds come in the fall, stay all winter, and move north again in spring. Average dates for these "winter residents" (WR), are similarly given. Finally, some birds come north in the spring and, after staying a while, continue northward. These can be seen only for a few weeks in spring and on their way south in the fall. These birds are "transients" (Tr). Approximate dates for all birds are given in abbreviated form: E, M, and L stand for "early," "middle," and "late." "E-Apr" means early April and "M-Oct" stands for middle October.

Always remember that local weather and other factors influence arrival and departure of birds. After several years, your own personal records may prove a better local guide than the abbreviated data given here, especially if you check dates with other local observers.

Page	Name	Migration		Eggs	
		Arrive	Depart	Size (in.)	No.
21	Common Loon	DC M-Oct B L-Sept SF M-Oct	WR M-May WR L-May WR E-May	3.5×2.2 Variable; greenish or dull brown with faint black spots.	2
22	Pied-billed Grebe	DC L-Mar B E-Apr StL M-Mar P Permanent Resident	SR L-Oct SR M-Oct SR L-Nov	1.7×1.1 Very light blue-green, darker or buff; unmarked.	4-8
23	Great Blue Heron	NY E-Apr B E-Apr StL L-Mar SF Permanent Resident	SR L-Nov SR M-Nov SR L-Oct	2.4×1.8 Pale bluish green to dull blue; unmarked.	3-4
24	Green Heron	DC M-Apr B L-Apr StL M-Apr SF M-Apr	SR L-Sept SR M-Sept SR L-Sept SR M-Sept	1.5×1.1 Pale greenish or greenish blue; unmarked.	3-6
25	Black-crowned Night Heron	B L-Mar StL L-Mar SF Permanent Resident P M-May	SR L-Nov SR E-Oct SR L-Sept	2.1×1.4 Pale bluish green.	3-5
26	American Bittern	DC L-Mar NY M-Apr StL E-Apr P M-Apr	SR E-Nov SR L-Oct SR L-Oct SR M-Oct	2×1.5 Greenish, shading into buff; unmarked.	3-5
27	Canada Goose	DC M-Oct B L-Sept StL E-Oct P M-Sept	WR M-Apr Tr L-Apr WR M-Apr WR M-May	3.4×2.3 Cream to dull greenish white. Later buffy and mottled.	4-10
28	Mallard	DC E-Nov NY L-Oct StL M-Sept P Permanent Resident	WR M-Apr WR M-Apr WR L-Mar	2.3×1.6 Pale greenish to grayish buff.	6-12
29	Black Duck	DC Permanent Resident NY Permanent Resident B Permanent Resident StL L-Oct	 WR E-Apr	2.3×1.7 Grayish white to greenish buff. Similar to Mallard.	6-12
30	Wood Duck	DC L-Feb NY M-Mar StL M-Feb P Permanent Resident	SR L-Nov SR E-Nov SR M-Nov	2×1.6 Dull cream to buff.	8-15

Nests		Food
Materials	Location	
Vegetable debris.	On ground, in hollows. Near shore, lake or pond.	Mainly fish; crabs, some insects and marine algae.
Decaying vegetation.	In shallow water. Floating among rushes in lakes and ponds.	Crayfish, crustaceans, small fish, and insects.
Sticks.	High up in tree or cliff near water.	Mainly fish; also crustaceans, frogs, and mice.
Sticks and twigs.	In trees, but near water; occasionally on ground.	Mainly fish, aquatic insects and crustaceans.
Sticks, twigs, and rushes.	In trees or rushes, in wooded swamps or islands.	Crayfish, fish, frogs, crabs, and insects.
Grasses and reeds.	On ground in marshes or wet grassy meadows.	Insects, frogs, crustaceans, fish; also mice.
Twigs, weeds, grasses, lined with down.	On dry ground near water.	Pondweeds, grasses; seeds of wheat, barley, sedges.
Reeds and grasses, lined with down.	On ground among high grass or reeds; usually near water.	Pondweeds, wild rice and other seeds; aquatic insects.
Grasses, weeds, leaves; feather lining.	Usually on ground in grass or brush. Often far from water.	Same as Mallard.
Grasses, twigs, leaves; down-lined.	Up to 60 ft. above ground; in a hole in tree or stump.	Wild rice, pondweeds, acorns, seeds, and fruits; some insects.

Page	Name	Migration		Eggs	
		Arrive	Depart	Size (in.)	No.
31	Pintail	NY M-Sept StL L-Sept SF E-Sept P Permanent Resident	WR M-Apr Tr L-Apr WR M-Mar	2.2×1.5 Similar to Mallard.	5-12
32	Canvasback	DC M-Oct NY M-Oct StL E-Mar SF M-Oct	WR L-Mar WR M-Apr Tr M-Dec WR L-Apr	2.5×1.6 Olive gray or dull green.	6-10
33	Common Merganser	DC L-Oct NY L-Oct B M-Oct P Permanent Resident	WR M-Apr WR L-Apr WR L-Apr	2.5×1.7 Pale buff; unmarked.	6-17
34	American Coot	DC E-Oct NY E-Oct StL M-Feb SF Permanent Resident	WR M-May WR L-Apr SR M-Nov	1.9×1.3 Light buff, speckled with dark brown or black.	•8-12
35	Killdeer	NY M-Mar B L-Mar StL E-Mar SF Permanent Resident	SR E-Nov SR L-Oct SR L-Nov	1.5×1.1 Buff or darker; heavily spotted or mottled.	4
36	Common Snipe	DC M-Sept StL L-Feb SF M-Sept P Permanent Resident	Tr L-Apr Tr L-Nov WR E-May	1.6×1.2 Pale olive to brown; darker spots and specks.	4
37	Greater Yellowlegs	DC E-Apr NY E-Apr StL E-Apr SF E-Aug	Tr E-Nov Tr E-Nov Tr L-Oct Tr L-May	1.4×1.2 Grayish white; blotched with purple and brown.	3-4
38	Spotted Sandpiper	DC M-Apr B E-May StL M-Apr P L-Apr	SR L-Sept SR M-Sept SR E-Oct SR M-Oct	1.3×.9 White to cream; heav- ily marked with dark brown and black.	4
39	Least Sandpiper	DC E-May StL L-Apr SF L-July P E-May	Tr M-Oct Tr L-Oct WR L-Apr Tr L-Sept	1.2×.8 Pale brown or gray; marked with brown, gray, or black.	3-4
40	Herring Gull	DC M-Sept NY L-Aug StL M-Oct SF E-Nov	WR M-May WR L-May WR L-Apr WR M-Apr	2.9×1.9 Variable. Whitish to gray or brown; brown spots and blotches.	3-4

Nests		Food
Materials	Location	
Straw, grass, rushes; lined with down.	On dry ground in the open.	Rushes, pondweeds, seeds of aquatic plants; molluscs and insects.
Reeds, lined with down.	On ground in reeds or rushes, near water.	Wild celery, pondweeds and other aquatic plants; some molluscs, and aquatic insects.
Leaves, grasses, moss; lined with down.	On ground; beneath bushes and between boulders; or in a hole in a tree.	Fish, crayfish, frogs, occasional aquatic insects.
Heaps of reeds, rushes, and coarse grass.	On ground near water; sometimes half afloat.	Duckweeds and other aquatic plants. Molluscs, crustaceans, and aquatic insects.
Slight depression lined with pebbles, grasses, or debris.	A hollow in ground, in pastures or fields.	Mainly insects and earthworms; small crustaceans.
Slight depression lined with grass.	On ground or on slight elevation in meadows, open marshes, or bogs.	Insects, crustaceans, worms, seeds of swamp and aquatic plants.
Slight depression with little or no lining.	On ground along shores and in marshes.	Small fish, snails, worms, crustaceans, and some insects.
Slight depression lined with grasses.	On ground or cavity in rocks, on sandy or rocky shores. Banks of streams and open upland fields.	Mainly insects; worms, spiders, and small crustaceans.
Slight depression, sparingly lined with grass.	On ground or rock in grassy lowlands near water. Sometimes on moist upland.	Aquatic insects, worms, and small crustaceans.
Seaweeds; marsh plants, chips, feathers, shells. Sometimes no nest.	On ground. Birds nest in colonies. Often on islands; sometimes under heavy vegetation.	Small fish, molluscs, crustaceans, insects, garbage, blueberries.

Page	Name	Migration		Eggs	
		Arrive	Depart	Size (in.)	No.
41	Common Tern	DC M-Apr NY L-Apr B E-May SF L-Apr	SR M-Oct SR M-Oct SR E-Oct SR M-Oct	1.6×1.2 2-3 Variable. Dull greenish white to brown; darker spots.	
42	Cooper's Hawk	NY M-Apr B M-Apr StL E-Apr SF Permanent Resident	Tr E-Oct SR E-Oct SR L-Oct	1.9×1.6 3-6 Bluish or greenish white; unmarked to heavily spotted with brown.	
43	Red-tailed Hawk	Permanent Resident throughout its range, except in north central states		2.6×1.8 2-4 Dull or creamy white; spotted brown or purple; rarely unmarked.	
44	Turkey Vulture	DC Permanent Resident NY L-Mar SF M-Mar P M-Mar	SR M-Nov SR L-Nov SR L-Sept	2.8×1.9 1-3 Dull white or buff; irregular brown spots.	
45	Sparrow Hawk	Permanent Resident throughout its range, except in north central states		1.3×1.2 4-7 White or tinted with buff; spotted or speckled with brown.	
46	Bald Eagle	Permanent Resident throughout its range		2.9×3.5 1-4 White; unmarked.	
47	Osprey	DC M-Apr B L-Apr StL E-Apr SF M-Mar	SR M-Oct SR E-Oct SR L-Oct SR M-Oct	2.5×1.8 2-4 Variable. Dull white to buff or light brown with brown blotches.	
48	Ring-necked Pheasant	Permanent Resident throughout its range		1.8×1.4 6-16 Buff to dark olive; occasionally greenish.	
49	Ruffed Grouse	Permanent Resident throughout its range		1.5×1.1 8-14 Pale buff but varying in color; unmarked.	
50	Bobwhite	Permanent Resident throughout its range		1.2×1.0 10-24 White; unmarked.	

Nests		Food
Materials	Location	
Hollow, lined with shells, to well-built mound of grass and seaweed.	On sand or bare rock, sometimes among grasses. Usually on islands.	Feeds almost wholly on small fish, but also some insects.
Branches and twigs; often lined with bark.	Usually in trees: pines preferred, 25-65 ft. high. Rarely on ground.	Mainly wild birds and poultry; some mammals; other vertebrates and insects.
Branches and twigs; lined with grasses, weeds, dead leaves.	In tall trees, 20-80 ft. up; in forest areas or in small groves.	Mainly rodents; some reptiles and poultry.
None.	On ground, rock ledge, or hollow log in secluded places, near water or in woods.	Carrion.
No nest material, unless some was left by previous occupant.	In cavity of tree, cliff embankment, 7-80 ft. up; often in farms or orchards.	Largely insects, some rodents, lizards, and small birds.
Large nest of branches and sticks. Additions and repairs are made yearly.	In treetops or cliffs; 30-90 ft. up; in forested or wooded regions, near streams, lakes, or ocean.	Mostly fish; some rodents and a few birds.
Platform of sticks; additions made from year to year.	In trees: 15-50 ft. up or on rocks. Ospreys nest along coasts.	Almost entirely fish.
Dead leaves, grass, straw.	On ground in bushy pastures, moorlands, grass, and grain fields.	Corn, wheat, barley, wild fruits, and insects.
Shallow depression, lined with leaves.	On ground, at base of tree in wooded uplands or dense thicket; under logs.	Leaves, buds, and fruits of forest plants. Occasional insects.
Grass, stems, strips of bark.	On ground in grass tangles, open fields, hedgerows.	Corn and grain. Ragweed, lespedeza, acorns, and weed seeds.

Page	Name	Migration		Eggs	
		Arrive	Depart	Size (in.)	No.
51	Pigeon	Permanent Resident throughout its range		1.5×1.1 White; unmarked.	2-3
52	Mourning Dove	DC Permanent Resident NY M-Mar SR M-Nov B L-Mar SR L-Oct SF L-Mar SR M-Nov		1.1×.8 White; unmarked.	2
53	Screech Owl	Permanent Resident throughout its range		1.4×1.3 White; unmarked.	3-5
54	Barn Owl	Permanent Resident throughout its range		1.6×1.2 White; unmarked.	5-11
55	Great Horned Owl	Permanent Resident throughout its range		2.3×1.9 Rough white; unmarked.	2-3
56	Yellow-billed Cuckoo	DC E-May SR M-Sept NY E-May SR L-Sept StL L-Apr SR L-Sept SF L-May SR E-Aug		1.2×.9 Light bluish green; unmarked; occasionally mottled.	2-4
57	Chimney Swift	DC M-Apr SR E-Oct B L-Apr SR E-Sept StL E-Apr SR M-Oct		.8×.5 White; unmarked.	4-5
58	Whip-poor-will	DC M-Apr SR L-Sept B E-May SR M-Sept StL M-Apr SR E-Oct		1.2×.8 Creamy white; spotted with brown.	2
59	Common Nighthawk	DC E-May SR L-Sept B M-May SR M-Sept StL L-Apr SR E-Oct P E-June SR L-Sept		1.2×.9 Dull white; spotted with gray and brown.	2
60	Ruby-throated Hummingbird	DC E-May SR L-Sept NY M-May SR M-Sept StL L-Apr SR E-Oct		.5×.4 White; unmarked.	2

Nests		Food
Materials	Location	
Sticks, straw, and debris.	Building (30 ft. and higher), on sheltered eaves or ledge.	Corn, oats, weed seeds, farm gleanings.
Stems, straws, sometimes leaves and moss.	In trees (pines preferred) 2-45 ft. above ground; in upland, sometimes in wet lowlands.	Wheat, corn, grass, and weed seeds.
No nest; or uses any available material.	Hollow of tree (5-50 ft. up), cranny, nook of building.	Rodents, small birds, frogs, fish, and insects.
Sometimes rubbish or debris. Usually no nest.	Underground in burrows or holes in embankments. Or elevated nests of other birds; steeples, barns.	Mice, rats, gophers, and some birds.
Sometimes uses old hawk nests; sometimes none.	In large trees (preferably pines) 10-90 ft. up. Sometimes in tree hollow or even on ground.	Rabbits, squirrels, rats, wild birds and poultry.
Sticks, rootlets, straws, pine needles, lichens.	In trees or thickets, 3-20 ft. up. Prefers margins of woods, orchards, or thickets.	Insects, mostly caterpillars, including hairy species.
Coarse twigs, held together by saliva of bird.	Usually near top of chimneys or rarely in barns or sheds; sometimes inside wells.	Flies, mosquitoes, and other small insects, caught in flight.
No nest construction. Uses slight depression in leaves.	On ground, usually in brushy wood margins, on well-drained land.	Moths, flying ants, and other insects caught in flight.
None. Eggs laid on bare surface.	On ground, rock, or on flat roofs of building; in open fields, pastures, or city lots.	Similar to Whip-poor-will.
Plant-down, bits of lichen outside; bound by threads of saliva and spider web.	Placed or "saddled" on branch of tree—3-50 ft. above ground.	Nectar of flowers and small insects.

Page	Name	Migration		Eggs	
		Arrive	Depart	Size (in.)	No.
61	Belted Kingfisher	DC L-Mar B E-Apr StL L-Feb SF M-Mar	SR E-Nov SR L-Oct SR L-Nov SR M-Nov	1.3×1.0 Glossy white; unmarked.	5-8
62	Red-headed Woodpecker	DC Permanent Resident NY E-May StL E-Apr	Tr L-Sept SR E-Oct	$1.0 \times .8$ White; unmarked.	4-6
63	Yellow-shafted Flicker	DC Permanent Resident NY M-Mar B M-Apr SF Permanent Resident	SR L-Oct SR M-Oct	$1.1 \times .9$ Glossy white; unmarked.	5-9
64	Yellow-bellied Sapsucker	DC E-Oct B M-Apr StL M-Mar SF M-Oct	WR M-Apr Tr L-Oct Tr M-Nov WR M-Mar	$.9 \times .7$ Glossy white; unmarked.	5-7
65	Downy Woodpecker	Permanent Resident throughout its range		$.8 \times .6$ White; unmarked.	4-6
66	Eastern Kingbird	DC L-Apr NY E-May StL M-Apr P M-May	SR E-Sept SR E-Sept SR M-Sept SR M-Sept	$1.0 \times .7$ Creamy white, spotted with brown.	3-4
67	Great Crested Flycatcher	DC E-May B M-May StL E-May	SR M-Sept SR E-Sept SR M-Sept	$.9 \times .7$ Creamy, streaked with brown.	3-6
68	Eastern Phoebe	DC M-Mar NY M-Mar StL E-Mar	SR M-Oct SR M-Oct SR M-Oct	$.8 \times .6$ White; occasionally spotted with brown.	4-5
69	Least Flycatcher	DC E-May B E-May StL E-May	Tr M-Sept SR E-Sept Tr E-Oct	$.6 \times .5$ White; unmarked.	3-4
70	Horned Lark	Permanent Resident throughout its range		$.8 \times .6$ Dull white; speckled with brown or purple.	3-5

Nests		Food
Materials	Location	
Nest lined with fish-bones and scales, leaves, grass.	At end of burrow in bank or bluff. Usually not more than 10 ft. up. Usually near water.	Mainly fish; some crustaceans and frogs.
A gourd-shaped hole, padded with chips.	Excavations in trees, posts, poles: 5-80 ft. up.	Beetles, ants, other insects. Acorns, other wild fruits and seeds.
Hole, padded with chips.	Cavity 10-24 in. deep in trees, snags, poles: 6 in.-60 ft. high.	Ants, beetles, and other insects. Wild fruits and seeds.
Hole, lined with chips.	Cavity in dead or live tree 8-40 ft. up; in woods or orchards.	Ants, beetles, other insects and their eggs. Wood and sap; wild fruits.
Gourd-shaped excavation: 6-10 in. deep.	In dead limb 5-50 ft. up; woodlands, orchards.	Ants and boring insects, spiders, snails. Some fruits and seeds.
Rootlets, grass, twine, hair, wool. Lined with fine grass, moss.	On horizontal limb of tree; bushes, eaves, fence rails, bridges: 2-60 ft. up.	Bees, ants, grasshoppers, beetles, etc. Also some wild fruits.
Twigs, grass, leaves, moss, feathers, and usually a cast-off snakeskin.	Cavity in dead limb or post. Sometimes buildings; 3-70 ft. up.	Moths, grasshoppers, other flying insects. Occasional fruits.
Of mud, covered with moss and dead leaves, lined with grass rootlets, moss, feathers.	In shelter of undercut banks, tree roots, culverts, eaves, or inside farm buildings; 1-20 ft. up.	Flying insects: beetles, flies, moths, etc. Some wild fruit; few seeds.
Grasses, bark fibers, lined with feathers and other soft materials.	Fork of tree or upright twigs: 2-60 ft. up. Usually along wood margins.	Small insects: flies, mosquitoes, moths, beetles.
Depression, loosely filled with grass, fibers, feathers.	On ground, in cultivated fields, sand dunes, or barren islands; in cover of grass and moss.	Mixed diet of insects and (in winter) seeds of weeds and grasses.

Page	Name	Migration		Eggs	
		Arrive	Depart	Size (in.)	No.
71	Purple Martin	DC L-Mar NY M-Apr StL L-Mar	SR M-Sept Tr L-Aug SR M-Sept	$1.0 \times .7$ White; unmarked.	4-5
72	Tree Swallow	DC M-Apr B M-Apr StL M-Mar SF E-Mar	Tr L-Sept SR M-Sept SR E-Oct SR M-Sept	$.7 \times .6$ White; unmarked.	4-7
73	Barn Swallow	NY M-Apr StL E-Apr SF L-Mar P M-Apr	SR M-Sept SR E-Oct SR E-Sept SR L-Sept	$.8 \times .5$ White, spotted with brown.	3-6
74	Black-billed Magpie	Permanent Resident throughout its range		$1.3 \times .9$ Grayish, heavily marked with brown.	4-8
75	Common Crow	Permanent Resident throughout its range		1.6×1.2 Variable. Pale greenish or bluish, spotted or blotched with brown.	3-5
76	Blue Jay	Permanent Resident throughout its range		$1.1 \times .9$ Greenish to olive, spotted with brown.	4-6
77	White-breasted Nuthatch	Permanent Resident throughout its range		$.8 \times .6$ White, rarely pinkish; speckled or spotted with brown.	5-8
78	Black-capped Chickadee	Permanent Resident throughout its range		$.6 \times .5$ White, finely spotted with brown.	5-8
79	Tufted Titmouse	Permanent Resident throughout its range		$.7 \times .6$ White to buff; speckled with grayish brown.	5-8
80	Brown Creeper	DC E-Oct NY L-Sept StL L-Sept SF Permanent Resident	WR L-Apr WR E-May WR L-Apr	$.6 \times .5$ White, speckled with brown.	5-8

Nests		Food
Materials	Location	
Leaves, grass, straw, twigs.	In cavities of trees, holes in cliffs: 3-30 ft. high. Frequently uses birdhouses.	Flying insects: flies, bees, beetles, flying ants, moths, etc.
Grass, lining of feathers.	Hollows and cavities in trees, woodpecker holes, crevices in buildings; also birdhouses; 2-50 ft. up.	Flies, moths, bees, beetles and other flying insects. Uses bayberries as a winter food.
Mud reinforced with plant material. Lined with feathers.	Commonly in barns; hollows in trees, cliffs; 5-20 ft. up. Adheres to an upright surface.	Entirely flying insects: flies, bees, ants, beetles.
Large nest of sticks and mud; lining of rootlets or horsehair.	In bushes and trees: 8-30 ft. up.	Grasshoppers; other insects, carrion, small mammals; wild and cultivated fruits.
Twigs and sticks, lined with rootlets, vines, grass.	In trees (preferably pine woods), height 10-70 ft.	Corn and other grains, weed seeds, wild fruits; grasshoppers and other insects.
Twigs and rootlets, lined with grass, feathers.	In a fork of tree: 5-50 ft. up. Prefers evergreen forests. But often in suburbs, farms, and villages.	Acorns, beechnuts, corn and other grain. Some insects, eggs, and young birds.
Grass, plant fibers, twigs, hair, and feathers.	A cavity or deserted woodpecker hole: 5-60 ft. up. Mature trees preferred.	Beetles, ants, other insects and their eggs. A few seeds.
Moss, hair, feathers, grass; lined with plant down.	Cavity in rotted stump or limb: 1-50 ft. up; or deserted woodpecker hole.	Insects and their eggs, weed and tree seeds; wild fruits.
Leaves, moss, bark; lined with feathers.	Deserted woodpeckers' holes or stumps: 2-85 ft. up.	Ants, bugs, and other insects; some seeds and fruits.
Twigs, plant fibers; sometimes lined with spider web feathers, or hair.	In trees, behind or between loose strip of bark: 5-15 ft. up. Usually in deep woods.	Mainly insects: beetles, bugs, caterpillars, ants, etc.

Page	Name	Migration		Eggs	
		Arrive	Depart	Size (in.)	No.
81	House Wren	DC M-Apr NY L-Apr StL M-Apr SF E-Mar	SR M-Oct SR E-Oct SR M-Oct SR M-Sept	.7×.5 Dull white, densely spotted with brown.	5-10
82	Mockingbird	DC Permanent Resident StL E-Mar SR L-Oct SF M-Sept WR M-Apr (Permanent Res. in S. Calif.)		1.0×.8 Greenish to blue; spot- ted brown, mostly at large end.	3-6
83	Catbird	DC L-Apr NY E-May StL L-Apr	SR M-Oct SR E-Oct SR M-Oct	.9×.7 Deep greenish blue or bluish green; unmarked.	4-6
84	Brown Thrasher	DC E-Apr NY L-Apr B L-Apr StL M-Mar	SR L-Sept SR L-Sept SR M-Sept SR E-Oct	1.1×.8 Grayish or greenish white; thickly spotted with brown.	3-6
85	Robin	DC Permanent Resident NY E-Mar SR M-Nov StL Permanent Resident SF E-Nov WR L-Mar		1.2×.8 Greenish blue; rarely spotted.	3-5
86	Wood Thrush	NY E-May B M-May StL M-Apr	SR E-Oct SR M-Sept SR M-Oct	1.1×.8 Bright greenish blue; unmarked.	3-5
87	Hermit Thrush	DC L-Oct NY E-Apr B M-Apr SF M-Oct	WR L-Apr SR M-Nov SR E-Nov WR E-Apr	.9×.7 Greenish blue; un- marked.	3-4
88	Eastern Bluebird	DC Permanent Resident NY M-Mar SR M-Nov StL L-Feb SR L-Nov P Permanent Resident		.9×.7 Pale blue; rarely white; unmarked.	4-6
89	Blue-gray Gnatcatcher	DC M-Apr NY L-Apr StL L-Mar SF Permanent Resident	SR E-Sept SR E-Sept SR M-Sept	.6×.5 White or bluish white; speckled with brown.	4-5
90	Ruby-crowned Kinglet	NY E-Apr B M-Apr StL E-Oct P M-Apr	Tr M-Oct Tr M-Oct Tr L-Apr SR M-Oct	.5×.4 White to cream. Sim- ilar to Golden-crowned Kinglet.	4-9

Nests		Food
Materials	Location	
Twigs, stems, grasses, lined with feathers, hair.	A cavity in hollow tree: 5-60 ft. up. Woodlands, farmyards, and in cities. Bird boxes commonly used.	Small insects: bugs, beetles, caterpillars, etc.
Bulky nest of coarse twigs, weed stems, shreds, string, rags.	In shrubs, thickets, vines; near houses; 1-15 ft., rarely higher.	Beetles, grasshoppers, and other insects; some wild fruit in season—grape and holly preferred.
Twigs and leaves. Lined with bark shreds, rootlets.	In shrubbery, thicket· 1-10 ft. and rarely 25 ft. high. Prefers dense lowlands.	Food similar to Mockingbird.
Bulky nest of coarse twigs, weed stalks, leaves. Lined with rootlets, grass.	In bushes, vines, brush, and low trees. Height: 0-12 ft.	Beetles, grasshoppers, caterpillars, etc. Also some acorns and wild fruit.
Mud wall and bottom, reinforced with grass, twine, twigs. Lined with grass.	In tree crotch or among branches. 5-70 ft. up. In woods or open country. On buildings, in rural areas.	Garden and field insects, worms; cultivated and wild fruits. Some seeds.
Leaves, rootlets, fine twigs. Firmly woven, with inner wall of mud.	Usually in saplings in woods. Height: 3-40 ft.	Beetles, ants, caterpillars, and other insects. Some wild fruits and weed seeds.
Moss, grasses, leaves. Lined with rootlets and pine needles.	On or near ground in pine or hemlock woods.	Food similar to Woodthrush.
Grasses, rootlets, hair, and some feathers.	In hollow trees, deserted woodpecker holes, and birdhouses. Height: 3-30 ft.	Many insects, including beetles, weevils, and grasshoppers. Also holly, dogwood, and other wild fruits.
Tendrils, fine bark, and grasses. Firmly woven and covered with lichens.	On a branch or in a crotch in tree near water. Height: 10-70 ft.	Mainly small insects: beetles, flies, caterpillars, moths.
Plant down, covered by mosses and lichens. Bound with plant fibers.	In conifers, often saddled on a limb; 5-50 ft. up.	Ants, plant lice, scale insects, and insect eggs. Occasional use of wild fruits.

Page	Name	Migration		Eggs	
		Arrive	Depart	Size (in.)	No.
91	Golden-crowned Kinglet	DC L-Sept NY L-Sept StL L-Mar SF L-Oct	WR M-Apr WR M-Apr Tr L-Oct WR E-Mar	.6×.4 White to cream; spotted with pale brown.	5-10
92	Cedar Waxwing	DC M-Sept NY M-May P Permanent Resident	WR E-June SR M-Nov	.9×.6 Grayish blue; speckled brown or black; mostly at large end.	3-5
93	Loggerhead Shrike	NY E-Aug B M-Mar StL Permanent Resident SF Permanent Resident	Tr E-Oct Tr L-Oct	1.0×.8 Dull white; spotted and blotched with light brown.	3-5
94	Starling	Permanent Resident throughout its range, except in extreme North		1.2×.9 Whitish or pale blue; unmarked.	4-6
96	Yellow Warbler	DC L-Apr NY E-May StL L-Apr SF M-Apr	SR E-Sept SR L-Aug SR M-Sept SR E-Sept	.7×.5 Pale bluish white; brown spots forming ring at larger end.	4-5
96	Black-and-White Warbler	DC M-Apr NY M-May StL M-Apr	SR L-Sept SR M-Sept SR L-Sept	.7×.5 Greenish white to buff; spotted and blotched with brown.	4-5
96	Blackthroated Blue Warbler	NY E-May B M-May StL E-May	Tr L-Sept Tr M-Sept Tr M-Sept	.7×.5 Creamy white; speckled with brown and lavender; mostly at larger end.	3-5
98	Yellowthroat	DC L-Apr NY E-May StL M-Mar SF Permanent Resident	SR E-Oct SR M-Oct SR E-Oct	.7×.5 Creamy white; speckled with brown and black; chiefly at large end.	3-5
98	Ovenbird	DC L-Apr NY E-May StL L-Apr	SR L-Sept SR M-Sept SR E-Oct	.8×.6 White, spotted with brown, especially at larger end.	4-6
98	Waterthrush	DC E-May B M-May StL L-Apr	Tr M-Sept Tr E-Sept Tr L-Sept	.8×.6 White to creamy; spotted with brown and gray.	4-5

	Nests	Food
Materials	*Location*	
Green mosses, lined with fine inner bark, black rootlets, and feathers.	In coniferous trees, partly suspended from twigs: 4-60 ft. up.	Insects: flies, beetles, plant lice; insect eggs.
Bulky nest of bark, leaves, grasses, rootlets, moss, and sometimes mud.	Often in fruit and shade trees at height of 5-50 ft.	Wild and cultivated fruits: grapes, dogwood, hawthorn, cherries; some insects.
Strips of bark, small twigs, and vegetable fibers; lined with grasses.	In thorny hedges or low trees: 5-20 ft. up.	Insects; grasshoppers, beetles; some small rodents and birds.
Large, poorly built nest of grasses and twigs.	In hollow of tree or crevice of building; 3-40 ft. high. Uses bird boxes.	Beetles, grasshoppers, and other insects; wild and cultivated fruits and grain.
Fine grasses and fibers; lined with plant down, fine grass, some hair.	In shrubs and trees: 3-8 ft. up. Rarely 40 ft. Fields and orchards, near water.	Caterpillars, weevils, and other small insects. Slight amount of plant food.
Strips of fine bark, grasses; lined with rootlets or hairs.	On ground, at base of trees, logs, or rocks.	Plant lice, caterpillars, beetles, scale and other insects.
Bark, fine grasses, pine needles. Lining of black rootlets.	In heavy undergrowth of dense woods: 1-10 ft. above ground.	Mainly insects: caterpillars, small beetles, plant lice, etc.
Bark, coarse grasses, dead leaves. Lined with fine grass tendrils.	On or near ground. Usually in clump of grass, in moist location.	Insects: cankerworms, weevils, leafhoppers, caterpillars, etc.
Bulky, covered nest. Entrance at one side. Of leaves, coarse grasses, and rootlets.	On leaf-covered ground in open woods.	Beetles, grasshoppers, and other ground insects. Worms and spiders.
Moss, lined with tendrils and fine rootlets.	On ground in a mossy bank or under roots of fallen tree.	Insects: beetles, bugs, caterpillars, leafhoppers, and spiders.

Page	Name	Migration		Eggs	
		Arrive	Depart	Size (in.)	No.
100	Myrtle Warbler	NY L-Sept StL E-Apr SF L-Oct	WR E-May Tr L-Oct WR M-Apr	.7 × .5 White, speckled with brown; often forming ring at larger end.	4-5
100	American Redstart	DC L-Apr B E-May StL L-Apr	SR M-Sept SR M-Sept SR M-Sept	.7 × .5 Bluish white; brown spots occasionally ringing large end.	4-5
100	Wilson's Warbler	DC E-May NY M-May SF L-Mar	Tr L-Sept Tr M-Sept SR E-Sept	.7 × .5 White or pinkish; brown spots forming ring at larger end.	4-5
102	Red-eyed Vireo	NY M-May B M-May StL M-Apr P E-May	SR L-Sept SR M-Sept SR E-Oct SR L-Sept	.9 × .6 White, sparsely speckled with brown or black.	3-4
103	House Sparrow	Permanent Resident throughout its range		.9 × .6 White to dull brown; speckled with brown.	4-7
104	Bobolink	DC E-May B M-May StL E-May P L-May	Tr L-Sept SR M-Sept Tr L-Sept SR M-Sept	.9 × .6 Dull white; spotted and blotched with brown and gray.	4-7
105	Meadowlark	NY M-Mar B L-Mar StL M-Mar SF Permanent Resident	SR L-Oct SR L-Oct SR L-Oct	1.1 × .8 White; completely spotted and speckled with brown.	3-7
106	Brewer's Blackbird	StL M-Mar SF Permanent Resident P Permanent Resident	Tr E-Apr	1.0 × .8 Dull white; almost entirely spotted with brown and black.	4-7
107	Redwinged Blackbird,	DC M-Mar NY M-May StL E-Mar SF Permanent Resident	SR M-Nov SR L-Oct SR E-Nov	1.0 × .7 Bluish white; irregular spots and streaks of purple and black.	3-5
108	Baltimore Oriole	DC E-May NY M-May StL L-Apr	Tr E-Sept SR E-Sept SR E-Sept	.9 × .6 White; irregular streaks and blotches of brown and black.	4-6

Nests		Food
Materials	Location	
Plant fibers; lining of grasses.	Coniferous trees in heavy woods: 5-40 ft. high.	Mainly common insects, but takes poison ivy, bayberry, and other fruits in winter.
Bark, leafstalks, plant down. Firmly woven and lined with rootlets.	Usually in the crotch of a sapling: 3-30 ft. above ground, rarely higher.	Small insects: flies, beetles, moths, leafhoppers, etc.
Ball of grass and moss wrapped in leaves. Lined with fine rootlets.	On ground among bushes in swampy land.	Small insects, similar to other warblers. Makes slight use of plant food.
Strips of bark, paper, plant down. Firmly and smoothly woven. Lined with bark and tendrils.	Suspended from a forked branch: 3-75 ft. up.	Caterpillars, moths, bugs, beetles, and other insects; small amount of wild fruit.
Of any available material: string, straw, twigs, paper, etc.	In any available place: in buildings, structures, eaves. Height: over 5 ft.	Corn, oats, wheat, and other grain; weed seeds; some insects during spring and summer.
Nest of grasses, weed stems, and rootlets.	On ground in the tall meadow grasses.	Wild rice, cultivated grains, weed seeds, caterpillars and other insects.
Grasses and weeds; often arched over.	Usually on ground in grassy fields or meadows.	Grain and wild grass seeds, wild fruits, grasshoppers, and other insects.
Twigs and coarse grass. Lined with finer grass.	On ground or in shrubs or coniferous trees. Height: 0-10 ft.	Oats and other grain, weed seeds, some insects.
Coarse grasses and weeds. Lined with finer grass and rootlets.	Attached to low bushes, reeds; usually in swamps. Usually less than 15 ft. high.	Weed and marsh plant seeds, grain; some fruit and insects in season.
Grasses, plant fibers, hair, strings, etc. Firmly interwoven.	Hanging from end of branches in shade or fruit trees. Height: 10-90 ft.	Caterpillars, beetles, and other insects; wild and some cultivated fruits.

Page	Name	Migration		Eggs	
		Arrive	Depart	Size (in.)	No.
109	Common Grackle	DC L-Feb SR L-Nov NY E-Mar SR E-Nov StL E-Mar SR M-Nov		1.2×.8 3-7 Bluish white; speckled and spotted dark brown to black.	
110	Brown-headed Cowbird	DC E-Mar SR E-Nov NY M-Mar SR M-Oct StL E-Mar SR M-Nov P E-May SR L-Sept		.9×.7 4-5 White or bluish; heavily speckled with gray or brown.	
111	Scarlet Tanager	DC E-May SR L-Sept B M-May SR M-Sept StL L-Apr SR E-Oct		.9×.7 3-4 Pale greenish or bluish; speckled brown at larger end.	
112	Cardinal	Permanent Resident over much of its range		1.0×.7 3-4 Pale bluish white; finely spotted with reddish brown.	
113	Rose-breasted Grosbeak	DC E-May Tr L-Sept NY M-May SR M-Sept StL L-Apr SR E-Oct		.9×.7 4-5 Pale blue; spotted with brown.	
114	Indigo Bunting	DC L-Apr SR E-Oct B M-May SR M-Sept StL L-Apr SR E-Oct		.7×.6 3-4 Pale bluish white; unmarked.	
115	American Goldfinch	Permanent Resident		.7×.5 3-6 Pale bluish white; unmarked.	
116	Purple Finch	DC L-Oct WR M-Apr NY L-Mar Tr E-Nov StL L-Mar Tr E-Nov SF Permanent Resident		.8×.6 4-6 Blue; spotted and speckled with brown at larger end.	
117	House Finch	Permanent Resident		.8×.6 3-5 Pale blue, nearly white; thinly speckled with black.	
118	Rufous-sided Towhee	NY M-Apr SR E-Oct B L-Apr SR E-Oct StL L-Mar SR M-Oct		1.0×.7 4-5 White or pinkish; brown specks at large end.	

Nests		Food
Materials	*Location*	
Bulky, but compact. Of mud and coarse grasses; lined with finer grasses.	Nests in colonies, most often in coniferous trees; sometimes in bushes. Height: 5-80 ft.	Grain and weed seeds. Some wild fruit; beetles, grasshoppers, crickets, etc.
None added.	Eggs laid in nests of other birds. Usually 1 or 2 in any one nest.	Grain and weed seeds. Grasshoppers and other insects.
Fine twigs and weeds. Lined with vine tendrils and stems.	On horizontal limb, often near its end: 10-70 ft. up.	Mainly insects: ants, beetles, moths, caterpillars. Dogwood, blackberry, and other wild fruits.
Twigs, rootlets, strips of bark. Lined with grasses and rootlets.	In thick bushes or vines: 2-10 ft. high. Rarely up to 30 ft.	Grape, holly, blackberry; wild seeds and a good many kinds of insects.
Loose nest of fine twigs, weeds, rootlets.	In trees or bushes: 5-20 ft. high.	Insects, including beetles, caterpillars, ants, bees. Wild fruits when available.
Grasses, bits of dead leaves, bark; lined with fine grass, rootlets, hairs.	In crotch of bush or sapling: 1-10 ft. up. Rarely as high as 20 ft.	Diet mixed: caterpillars and other insects; some wild fruits, weed seeds.
Fine grasses, bark, moss; thickly lined with thistledown.	In trees or bushes: 5-35 ft. high.	Mainly weed seeds, grain, and wild fruit. Occasional plant lice and caterpillars.
Twigs, grasses, and rootlets. Thickly lined with hairs.	Woods, in pine and spruce trees: 5-60 ft. high.	Tree seeds and wild fruits. Some insects.
Rootlets and grasses. Lined with horsehair.	Trees, bushes, and vines: 5-20 ft. above ground. Often near buildings.	Weed seeds, tree seeds, plant lice and other insects.
Dead leaves and bark; lined with fine grasses.	Usually on ground; sometimes in bushes or saplings: 0-10 ft. high.	Wild fruits and weed seeds. Insects, worms, and spiders.

Page	Name	Migration		Eggs	
		Arrive	Depart	Size (in.)	No.
119	Brown Towhee	Permanent Resident in its range		$1.0 \times .7$ Variable; bluish marked with purple and black.	3-4
120	Slate-colored Junco	DC E-Oct NY L-Sept P E-Oct	WR L-Apr WR L-Apr WR M-Mar	$.8 \times .6$ Pale bluish white; brown spots may form ring at larger end.	4-5
122	Field Sparrow	NY M-Apr B M-Apr StL L-Mar	SR L-Oct SR M-Oct SR E-Nov	$.7 \times .5$ White to pale blue or green; speckled with brown.	3-5
122	Tree Sparrow	NY E-Nov B L-Oct StL L-Oct P L-Oct	WR L-Mar WR E-Apr WR L-Mar WR M-Mar	$.8 \times .6$ Pale greenish or bluish green; speckled with light brown.	4-5
122	Vesper Sparrow	DC L-Mar B M-Apr StL L-Mar P E-Apr	SR L-Oct SR M-Oct Tr M-Nov SR M-Sept	$.9 \times .6$ Dull white; thickly spotted with brown.	4-5
124	Chipping Sparrow	DC L-Mar B M-Apr StL L-Mar SF M-Apr	SR E-Nov SR M-Oct SR L-Oct SR M-Sept	$.7 \times .5$ Greenish blue; speckled with brown, mostly at larger end.	4-5
124	White-crowned Sparrow	DC E-May NY M-May StL L-Apr Permanent Resident	Tr M-Nov Tr L-Oct Tr E-Nov	$.9 \times .6$ Bluish and greenish white, spotted with brown.	4-5
124	White-throated Sparrow	DC M-Oct NY E-Oct StL M-Oct	WR M-May Tr M-May Tr M-May	$.8 \times .6$ White to bluish; speckled and blotched with reddish brown.	4-5
126	Song Sparrow	Permanent Resident over much of its range		$.8 \times .6$ Variable. White or greenish; spotted and speckled with brown.	4-5
126	Swamp Sparrow	DC E-Oct B M-Apr StL L-Mar	WR E-May SR M-Oct Tr L-Oct	$.8 \times .6$ Bluish white; spotted or blotched with brown.	4-5
126	Fox Sparrow	DC L-Oct NY L-Oct StL L-Oct SF E-Oct	Tr L-Mar Tr E-Apr Tr E-Apr WR E-Apr	$.8 \times .6$ Greenish white; spotted with dull brown.	4-5

Nests		Food
Materials	**Location**	
Grasses, weeds, and twigs. Lined with rootlets.	On ground or in low bushes. Less than 10 ft. high.	Oats and barley; weed seeds, caterpillars and other insects.
Grasses, moss, and rootlets. Lined with fine grass and hair.	On or very near ground in fallen tree, logs, upturned roots; under overhanging banks, along wood roads.	Ragweed, crabgrass, and other weed seeds. Some caterpillars and other insects.
Coarse grasses, weeds, rootlets. Lined with fine grass and hairs.	On ground or low bushes (10 ft. or less) in fields, overgrown pastures.	Similar to Tree Sparrow, with some use of grain.
Grasses, rootlets, and hair.	On ground or in stunted conifers near timberline; near water.	Largely weed seeds; crabgrass, pigweed, sedge, etc. Some insects eaten.
Coarse grass. Lined with finer grasses, rootlets, hairs.	On ground in dry upland fields; along dry roadsides.	Weed seeds of many kinds; some grain, and various insects.
Grasses, fine twigs, rootlets. Thickly lined with hair.	In trees or bushes; in shrubbery near houses. Height: 3-35 ft. Rarely on ground.	Weed seeds, oats, and timothy; leafhoppers and other common insects.
Grasses, moss, and rootlets. Lined with hair.	Usually on ground or in clump of grass in woods or thickets.	Ragweed, pigweed, knotweed, and other weed seeds; some grain and a number of kinds of insects.
Grasses, rootlets, moss, strips of bark. Lined with finer grasses.	Usually on ground in hedgerows and woodland undergrowth.	Food very similar to White-crowned Sparrow.
Nest of grasses and rootlets. Lined with fine grasses and hair.	On ground or in low bushes; in grass thickets or saplings. Up to 8 ft.; rarely 15 ft.	Food similar to that of Swamp Sparrow.
Coarse grasses, rootlets, dead leaves. Lined with finer grasses and sometimes hair.	On or close to ground; in grasses in wet meadow and marshes or swamps.	Seeds of weeds and grasses. Beetles, caterpillars, and other insects.
Coarse grasses. Lined with finer grasses, hair, mosses, feathers.	On ground or in low bushes; coniferous forests or alder thickets preferred.	Weed seeds, wild fruits, some grain, millipedes, and various insects.

MORE INFORMATION

PUBLICATIONS Here are a few of the best publications to help you in more advanced bird study:

Hickey, Joseph J., A GUIDE TO BIRD WATCHING, Oxford University Press, New York, 1954. A most helpful book, with practical details on what the amateur can do and how to do it.

McElroy, Thomas P., Jr., NEW HANDBOOK OF ATTRACTING BIRDS, Knopf, New York, 1960. Much about activities with birds.

Martin, A. C., Zim, H. S., and Nelson, A. L., AMERICAN WILDLIFE AND PLANTS, Dover, N. Y., 1961. Reprint of standard volume with data on food and feeding habits of many American birds.

Peterson, Roger T., A FIELD GUIDE TO THE BIRDS (eastern land and water birds), Houghton Mifflin Co., Boston, 1947; A FIELD GUIDE TO WESTERN BIRDS, Houghton Mifflin Co., Boston, 1961. Excellent guides, emphasizing field markings and outlines of birds in flight; standard references for birds watchers.

Pettingill, Olin Sewall, Jr., A GUIDE TO BIRD FINDING (East of the Mississippi), Oxford University Press, New York, 1951; A GUIDE TO BIRD FINDING (West of the Mississippi), Oxford University Press, New York, 1953. Guides to the exact localities where birds may be seen in abundance.

The Audubon Magazine, published by the National Audubon Society, 1130 Fifth Ave., New York, N. Y.

MUSEUMS AND ZOOS are good places to supplement your field study.

Albany: New York State Museum

Atlanta: Georgia State Museum

Cambridge, Mass.: Museum of Comparative Zoology, Harvard Univ.

Chicago: Chicago Natural History Museum; Brookfield Zoo

Denver: Denver Museum of Natural History

Gainesville (Fla.): Florida State Museum

Los Angeles: Los Angeles County Museum; Griffith Park (Zoo)

New Orleans: Louisiana State Museum; Audubon Park (Zoo)

New York: American Museum of Natural History; N. Y. Zoological Park

Philadelphia: Philadelphia Academy of Natural Sciences; Philadelphia Zoological Gardens

San Francisco: California Academy of Sciences; S. F. Zoological Gardens

Seattle: Washington State Museum

Washington, D.C.: U. S. National Museum; National Zoological Park

PLACES FOR STUDYING BIRDS

Listed here are some National Wildlife Refuges (NWR) and other areas famous for the number and variety of birds seen there.

Roadrunner (24 in.), a streaked, slender, swift bird. It rarely flies.

UNITED STATES

Alabama: Cochrane Bridge, Mobile. **Arizona:** Huachuca Mts., Tombstone. **Arkansas:** White River NWR, St. Charles. **California:** Tule-Klamath Basin, Tule Lake; Sacramento NWR, Willows; Yosemite Nat. Pk. **Colorado:** Rocky Mt. Nat. Pk. **Connecticut:** Audubon Nature Center, Greenwich. **Delaware:** Bombay Hook NWR, Smyrna. **Florida:** Everglades Nat. Pk., Homestead; St. Marks NWR, St. Marks. **Georgia:** Okefenokee NWR, Waycross. **Illinois:** Chautauqua NWR, Havana. **Louisiana:** Sabine NWR, Hackberry. **Maryland:** Ocean City area, Ocean City; Pocomoke River Swamp, Powellsville. **Massachusetts:** Parker River NWR, Newburyport; Monomoy NWR, South Chatham. **Michigan:** Seney NWR, Germfask. **Minnesota:** Itasca State Pk. **Nebraska:** Valentine NWR, Valentine. **New Hampshire:** Connecticut Lakes, Pittsburg. **New Jersey:** Cape May Point, Cape May. **New Mexico:** Bosque del Apache NWR, Socous. **New York:** Montauk Pt. State Pk., Montauk. **North Carolina:** Red Rock Lakes NWR, New Holland; Greenfield Pk., Wilmington. **North Dakota:** Des Lacs NWR, Kenmare. **Ohio:** Buckeye Lake, Hebron. **Oklahoma:** Wichita Mts. NWR, Lawton. **Oregon:** Malheur NWR, Burns; Netarts Bay, Netarts. **Pennsylvania:** Hawk Mt., Kempton. **Rhode Island:** Sakonnet Pt., Little Compton. **South Carolina:** Cape Romain NWR, McClellanville. **South Dakota:** Sand Lake NWR, Columbia; Black Hills. **Tennessee:** Great Smoky Mts. Nat. Pk., Gatlinburg; Reelfoot Lake, Tiptonville. **Texas:** Santa Ana and Laguna Atascosa NWR, San Benito; Rockport; Guadalupe Mts. **Utah:** Bear River Migratory Bird Refuge, Brigham City. **Vermont:** Missisquoi NWR, Swanton. **Virginia:** Back Bay NWR, Pungo; Dismal Swamp, Suffolk. **Washington:** Willipa Bay area, Wesport; Olympic Nat. Pk.; Mt. Rainier Nat. Pk. **Wisconsin:** Horicon NWR, Waupun. **Wyoming:** Yellowstone Nat. Pk.

CANADA

Manitoba: Riding Mt. Nat. Pk. **Ontario:** Algonquin Provincial Pk.; Point Pelee Nat. Pk. **Quebec:** Bonaventura Island.

SCIENTIFIC NAMES

Following are the scientific names of species illustrated in this book. The genus name is given first; the species name follows. The numbers in heavy type indicate the pages where species are illustrated.

16 Asyndesmus lewis.
18 Cyanocitta stelleri.
19 Icteria virens.
21 Gavia immer.
22 Podilymbus podiceps.
23 Ardea herodias.
24 Butorides virescens.
25 Nycticorax nycticorax.
26 Botaurus lentiginosus.
27 Branta canadensis.
28 Anas platyrhynchos.
29 Anas rubripes.
30 Aix sponsa.
31 Anas acuta.
32 Aythya valisineria.
33 Mergus merganser.
34 Fulica americana.
35 Charadrius vociferus.
36 Capella gallinago.
37 Totanus melanoleucus.
38 Actitis macularia.
39 Erolia minutilla.
40 Larus argentatus.
41 Sterna hirundo.
42 Accipiter cooperii.
43 Buteo jamaicensis.
44 Turkey: Cathartes aura.
   Black: Coragyps stratus.
45 Falco sparverius.
46 Haliaëtus leucocephalus.
47 Pandion haliaëtus.
48 Phasianus colchicus.
49 Bonasa umbellus.
50 Colinus virginianus.
51 Columbia livia.
52 Zenaidura macroura.
53 Otus asio.

54 Tyto alba.
55 Bubo virginianus.
56 Coccyzus americanus.
57 Chaetura pelagica.
58 Caprimulgus vociferus.
59 Chordeiles minor.
60 Archilochus colubris.
61 Megaceryle alcyon.
62 Melanerpes erythrocephalus.
63 Colaptes auratus.
64 Sphyrapicus varius.
65 Dendrocopus pubescens.
66 Tyrannus tyrannus.
67 Myiarchus crinitus.
68 Sayornis phoebe.
69 Empidonax minimus.
70 Eremophila alpestris.
71 Progne subis.
72 Iridoprocne bicolor.
73 Hirundo rustica.
74 Pica hudsonia.
75 Corvus brachyrhynchos.
76 Cyanocitta cristata.
77 Sitta carolinensis.
78 Parus atricapillus.
79 Parus bicolor.
80 Certhia familiaris.
81 Troglodytes aedon.
82 Mimus polyglottos.
83 Dumetella carolinensis.
84 Toxostoma rufum.
85 Turdus migratorius.
86 Hylocichla mustelina.
87 Hylocichla guttata.
88 Sialia sialis.
89 Polioptila caerulea.
90 Regulus calendula.

SCIENTIFIC NAMES (continued)

91 Regulus satrapa.
92 Bombycilla cedrorum.
93 Lanius ludovicianus.
94 Sturnis vulgaris.
95 Dendroica petechia.
97 Yellow: Dendroica petechia.
    Black-and-white: Mniotilta
      varia.
    Black-throated Blue:
      Dendroica caerulescens.
99 Yellowthroat: Geothlypis
      trichas.
    Ovenbird: Seiurus
      aurocapillus.
    Northern Waterthrush:
      Seiurus noveboracensis.
101 Myrtle: Dendroica coronata.
    American Redstart:
      Setophaga ruticilla.
    Wilson's: Wilsonia pusilla.
102 Vireo olivaceus.
103 Passer domesticus.
104 Dolichonyx oryzivorus.
105 Sturnella magna.
106 Euphagus cyanocephalus.
107 Agelaius phoeniceus.
108 Icterus galbula.
109 Quiscalus quiscula.
110 Molothrus ater.
111 Piranga olivacea.
112 Richmondena cardinalis.
113 Pheucticus ludovicianus.
114 Passerina cyanea.
115 Spinus tristis.
116 Carpodacus purpureus.
117 Carpodacus mexicanus.

118 Pipilo erythrophthalmus.
119 Pipilo fuscus.
120 Junco hyemalis.
121 Spizella passerina.
123 Field: Spizella pusilla.
    Tree: Spizella arborea.
    Vesper: Pooecetes
      gramineus.
125 Chipping: Spizella
      passerina.
    White-crowned: Zonotrichia
      leucophrys.
    White-throated: Zonotrichia
      albicollis.
127 Song: Melospiza melodia.
    Swamp: Melospiza
      georgiana.
    Fox: Passerella iliaca.
128 Arctic Tern: Sterna
      paradisaea.
    Snow Goose: Chen
      hyperborea.
    Ring-necked Duck: Aythya
      collaris.
129 Smith's Longspur: Calcarius
      pictus.
    Black Brant: Branta bernicla.
130 Varied Thrush: Ixoreus
      noevius.
    Pine Grosbeak: Pinicola
      enucleator.
    Common Egret:
      Casmerodius albus.
    Little Blue Heron: Florida
      coerulea.
155 Geococcyx californianus.

INDEX

Asterisks (*) denote pages on which birds are illustrated.

MEASURING SCALE (IN MILLIMETERS AND CENTIMETERS)